Helping with Behaviour

Helping with Behaviour shows how to establish good practice in early years settings, so that *all* children are supported in developing positive interactions with each other.

Sue Roffey explains the features of an 'emotionally literate' environment that meets the needs of more vulnerable children and looks at how to respond effectively when children are distressed and hard to manage, providing plenty of ideas and inspiration throughout.

Using accessible and down-to-earth language, this book looks at:

▶ how to foster a sense of belonging and build self-esteem;
▶ how we can help pre-schoolers learn to feel good about complying and cooperating;
▶ how children can become strong individuals as well as learn to be good;
▶ ways of working collaboratively to address the most challenging behaviours.

This book is based on sound psychological theory and research but written especially for early years practitioners, who will easily be able to engage with the ideas presented and hence develop strong principles of positive behaviour themselves. The wide range of concepts included here will be an invaluable source of inspiration, making this book essential reading for anyone concerned with vulnerable young children in their care.

Sue Roffey is a senior lecturer in educational psychology at the University of Western Sydney. She also works internationally providing consultancy and professional development on issues related to behaviour and emotional literacy. See www.sueroffey.com.

The Nursery World/Routledge Essential Guides for Early Years Practitioners

Books in this series address key issues for early years practitioners working in today's nursery and school environments. Each title is packed full of practical activities, support, advice and guidance, all of which is in line with current government early years policy. The authors use their experience and expertise to write accessibly and informatively, emphasising through the use of case studies the practical aspects of the subject, while retaining strong theoretical underpinnings throughout.

These titles will encourage the practitioner and student alike to gain greater confidence and authority in their day-to-day work, offering many illustrative examples of good practice, suggestions for further reading and many invaluable resources. For a handy, clear and inspirational guide to understanding the important and practical issues, the early years practitioner or student need look no further than this series.

Titles in the series

Circle Time for Young Children
Jenny Mosley

Helping with Behaviour: establishing the positive and addressing the difficult in the early years
Sue Roffey

Identifying Additional Learning Needs in the Early Years: listening to the children
Christine MacIntyre

Observing, Assessing and Planning for Children in the Early Years
Sandra Smidt

Encouraging Creative Play and Learning in the Early Years
(forthcoming)
Diane Rich

Helping with Behaviour

Establishing the Positive and Addressing the Difficult in the Early Years

Sue Roffey

Routledge
Taylor & Francis Group
LONDON AND NEW YORK

NURSERY
WORLD

First published 2006
by Routledge
2 Park Square, Milton Park, Abingdon, Oxon OX14 4RN

Simultaneously published in the USA and Canada
by Routledge
270 Madison Ave, New York, NY 10016

Routledge is an imprint of the Taylor & Francis Group

Typeset in Perpetua and Bell Gothic by
Florence Production Ltd, Stoodleigh, Devon
Printed and bound in Great Britain by
TJ International Ltd, Padstow, Cornwall

British Library Cataloguing in Publication Data
A catalogue for this book is available from the British Library

Library of Congress Cataloging in Publication Data
Roffey, Sue.
   Helping with behaviour: establishing the positive and addressing
   the difficult in the early years/Sue Roffey.
      p. cm
   The Nursery world/Routledge essential guides for early years practitioners
   Includes bibliographical references.
   1. Classroom management.   2. Behavior modification.   3. Preschool
   teaching.   4. Preschool children – Psychology.   5. Problem children –
   Education (Preschool)   I. Title.   II. Series.
   LB3013.R562 2005
   372.139'3 – dc22   2005004367

ISBN 0–415–34290–2 (hbk)
ISBN 0–415–34291–0 (pbk)

This book is dedicated to my dearest son Ben who is now working as a forensic psychologist, researching aspects of criminal behaviour. He, as much as anyone, has a deep understanding of the importance of positive intervention in the early years.

Contents

Preface

'Helping with behaviour' means helping the children, helping each other and helping with ideas. Here we explore how to establish good practice in early years settings so that all children are supported in developing the positive interactions on which pro-social behaviour is founded.

The book is aimed at those who work with 3–5-year-old children, although there are references to those a little younger and a little older. It is written for an international readership and as such does not refer to nation-specific or statutory information. Terminology varies between countries: in this book, the terms 'early years centre' and 'pre-school' apply to all establishments that cater for the 3–5 age group and the term 'pre-school practitioner' is applied to all people working in this field. The word 'teacher' refers to anyone with a responsibility in an early years setting even if they do not have the formal qualifications.

The approach here is rooted in developmental, educational and social psychology primarily from systemic, interactive and constructivist perspectives. Some psychodynamic, social learning and behavioural approaches are also included. There is an emphasis on solution-focused and strengths-based thinking. The content is informed by research, which concludes that the way we position children and their behaviour determines what we address and how we address it. We look at what parents and early years practitioners require of small children in different settings and how to help pre-schoolers learn what is wanted in ways that make them feel positive about complying and cooperating. It is important that practitioners are aware of what is developmentally appropriate in behavioural terms. We explain how children need to become strong individuals as well as 'learn to be good' and ways in which that might be fostered without resorting to 'strong discipline'.

The features of an emotionally literate environment are essential for all children but especially those who are more vulnerable. What this entails is explored, including ways of responding more effectively when children are distressed and hard to manage. There is a strong focus on modelling as well as teaching positive behaviour and on developing warm and responsive relationships, fostering belonging and building self-efficacy.

We are said to live in an increasingly violent, irresponsible and selfish society, where immediate gratification is the norm. There is certainly good evidence for many people being unhappy. The facts and figures about relationship breakdown, suicide and self-harm, depression and anxiety are indisputable. There is also much research evidence that points to the importance of early experiences in social and emotional development which underpin how people relate to each other and find coping strategies to manage difficult situations.

The experiences that small children and their families have in their first educational placement is crucial, especially if they are vulnerable and at risk. Although these cannot stand alone from all the other influences in society, they can make a significant difference to individuals by setting in train expectations for the future. This includes messages children and families receive about their potential for competence. Small things over time can make big differences. The early years practitioner in their everyday interactions and approaches can foster hopefulness. This book helps show you how.

Acknowledgements

I would like to thank the following people who made this book possible:

Sally Jeffrey, Lyn McPherson and Ambika Maharaj in Australia; Terry McKenzie in New Zealand; and Claire Witkowski and Priscilla Webster in the UK for their help in discussing issues, reading drafts and providing some of the case studies. I am grateful for their valuable time and expertise.

Lynley McNab, Julie Quinn and Natasha van der Wall for sharing their experiences and knowledge so generously. Chapter 5 on learning and language owes much to their input.

Christine Avenoso, Ian Birrell, Ashika Nand and Stephanie Ticli for sharing their insights on the positioning of 'hard to manage' children in early years centres, their experience as teachers and their developing understanding as school counsellors.

My family, as ever, for their continual support, help and love. They are the backbone of my endeavours. David's patience, good humour, encouragement and practical assistance is the calm oasis which maintains my own well-being.

The many families, teachers and other education professionals, children and students with whom I have had contact over the years and who have given me so much food for thought and examples of good practice. All names and details here have been changed to protect confidentiality.

Chapter 1

A privilege and a responsibility

The importance and skills of practitioners and good practice in early years settings are vital in reducing social exclusion. How we talk and think about children and their behaviour matters. Solution-focused, systemic and contextual approaches are more helpful. There are no quick fixes: it is the whole package over time that makes the difference and relationships are central. We need to work systemically, consistently and supportively. Social and emotional competence is central to a child's ability to achieve academically and to the development of socially responsible behaviour.

INTRODUCTION

More than at any other age, those who work with children in the early years hold the future in their hands and in their hearts. Research continually emphasizes the importance of the first few years of a child's life. Early experiences and relationships at home and in pre-school settings set the stage for the development of crucial competencies such as self-regulation, empathy and interpersonal skills – all of which impact on future relationships and how an individual functions in the world (National Research Council and Institute of Medicine 2000).

It is here, in the first few years of life, that children learn ways of interpreting experience – making sense of the world and themselves in it. These interpretations underpin patterns of responding that become more established with age. These include:

▶ The development of self-concept – how children come to see themselves.

1

▶ The development of self-esteem – whether or not they have positive feelings about themselves.
▶ The development of self-efficacy – whether they believe they can have an impact on their world.
▶ Their understanding of relationships – what they learn about others and their interactions with them.
▶ Their general conceptualizations of the world around them and the meanings that are given to various aspects of existence. This includes whether they see the world as an exciting place to explore or a scary place in which you either don't take risks or fight for survival.

What matters most is what the significant people in children's lives say and do. In this first instance these are the child's immediate carers, usually their family. We know, however, that a 'significant other' in a child's life is a major factor in their resilience (Raphael 2000). These people can be extended family members such as grandparents but can also include teachers. It is the quality of the relationship that is important. If a child has the experience of being valued and supported by someone they will know they have the potential for being lovable.

Relationship building and maintenance is integral throughout this book. We look at what behaviours might mean and how to respond with care and consistency to help children believe they are important and wanted – even when we are letting them know that their behaviour is unacceptable. We explore ways of helping children learn to think and feel about themselves positively and see cooperation as in their interests. We consider how to respond in developmentally sensitive ways that facilitate self-awareness and 'other' awareness. We honour each child's individuality and celebrate their strengths while helping them become more successful in their endeavours to learn and relate more effectively.

Those who work in the early years need to support the process of socialization, helping children become less egocentric and increasingly effective in a social world. Chapter 2 is about how young children come to understand what is required of them in behavioural terms. How do they learn what 'good' means and how can we help them begin to internalize pro-social values rather than just doing as they are told for fear of getting into trouble if they don't? How can we foster individual strengths but also ensure that qualities such as high energy, determination and independence are channelled into productive outcomes for the child and for others?

Chapter 3 provides practical guidance for teachers on what needs to be taken into consideration in promoting 'desired' behaviour, together with initial responses to children who are behaving in ways which are hurtful or unhelpful. The principles here apply to all children but especially those learning ways of being in pre-school settings which are different from the expectations at home. This guidance is congruent with and underpins responses to more distressed children.

Although it is threaded throughout the book, emotional literacy is the specific focus for Chapter 4. This looks at what is involved in constructing an ethos which is emotionally safe and where children feel they belong. We also explore practical ways of helping children develop the emotional competencies that enhance resilience.

Chapter 5 covers the developmental issues in the pre-school years that impact on understanding and learning. A high proportion of the children whose behaviour gives cause for serious concern in the early years have difficulties with cognition and/or communication and it is important to identify these and take appropriate action.

Responding with emotional literacy and professional integrity to those who have faced distressing events in their young lives is the focus of Chapter 6. This covers the more challenging and possibly entrenched situations where children have experienced loss, abuse or other trauma.

Chapter 7 begins by providing a framework for responding to a high level of emotion and then addresses specific behaviours that may be especially difficult or disturbing and how to gather good information to inform further assessments.

Chapter 8 addresses issues in working with families. Blaming stressed, under-resourced parents for lacking the knowledge and skills to respond effectively to their children is a road to nowhere. Conversations need to be solution focused and strengths based.

The final chapter focuses on helping early years professionals weather the inevitable struggles by looking after themselves and supporting each other. Promoting well-being for everyone is not just a warm and fuzzy idea – it makes all the difference to what is possible in maintaining good practice (Weare and Gray 2003).

WAYS OF THINKING ABOUT CHILDREN AND BEHAVIOUR

How we think about children, their families, our role and how we support each other all contribute to the hopefulness or helplessness we feel when faced with behaviour we find really hard to manage.

3

Often we see difficult behaviour as rooted within the child – what they can't or won't do. This way of thinking is referred to in various ways as:

▶ the 'medical' model: diagnose the problem and provide 'treatment';
▶ the 'within child' model: the problem exists within the child who needs to change;
▶ the 'individual deficit' or 'pathological' model: focusing on the child's faults and failures.

This way of thinking is not responsive to the whole child nor to the whole context in which behaviour is manifest. Although factors within the individual child might be part of a holistic response, by itself the medical model limits positives, possibilities and responsibilities. It also gives rise to a simplistic 'cause and effect' way of thinking when human beings and their situations are invariably much more complex. There is a danger within this model that children are seen to be deliberately difficult and challenging to adults rather than responding to experiences and needing support to develop pro-social behaviour.

Seeing children's behaviour as the family's fault is understandable and probably an even more common attribution. It is, however, no more useful than focusing entirely on the child.

We cannot do anything ourselves to change the child's family or history. We cannot change their personality or indeed any special needs they may have. All we can change are the approaches and contexts over which we have some control.

Change will happen as a result of how we think about an issue and what we do or don't do as an outcome of that thinking. This includes our own values and beliefs, how we understand the meaning of behaviours, how we determine what is in the child's best interests and what we need as practitioners. This guides what we might do individually and collaboratively to maximize optimal outcomes.

This book is written from the stance of theoretical models considered to be both more useful to practitioners and also more respectful and empowering to children and families. These are briefly summarized here.

Interactive systems theory (also referred to as eco-systemic theory)

Each individual is born with a different personality and a different potential. It is the interaction of this individuality with their environment that influences how they develop. Although the greatest influence on the child is their immediate daily caregivers, the way parents learn to be with their child comes from their own experiences, their extended family and their community. The support families receive from both friends and services impacts on how well they function as parents, as do family-friendly policies in the workplace. The laws of the country and the values and norms that underpin these are also powerful influences. Many of the issues that present difficulties are at the interface of different systems where adaptations are required to meet unfamiliar or incongruent expectations (Foot *et al.* 2004). This means that whether a family has the same or different values as their child's early years centre or school will impact on relationships (Bronfenbrenner 1979, 2004).

Changes both within and between systems have a ripple effect. If we focus on gaining success with one behaviour and acknowledge the child's achievements they may begin to think of themselves differently and behaviour may begin to improve in other areas. If we support rather than blame a struggling mother, she is less likely to feel stressed and more able to relate positively to her child, who will develop more optimally as a result. The same theory applies to early years practitioners. If individuals come into work knowing they are valued by their colleagues they are likely to have more emotional energy to relate to children effectively in challenging circumstances.

The eco-systemic model helps us to both reserve judgement on families and give confidence in knowing that what we do in our own settings may help make up for disadvantages elsewhere.

> *In certain ecologies, overarching forces, outside the control of parents, may entirely overwhelm the beneficial effects of authoritative parenting in the home. In other contexts, beneficial forces outside the family may offset what otherwise might be disastrous parenting.*
>
> (Steinberg *et al.* 1995: 461)

Social constructionist theory

This theory emphasizes the importance of meaning and how people have different 'realities' based in 'dominant discourses' or how people talk about things. A good example is the construct of 'success' in Western society. Most people do not question that success means getting a 'good' job, having money and enjoying status. This is presented by markets, media, and government policies, and perpetuated by conversations.

5

Success in other cultures or at other times in history is linked to different values, such as supporting the extended family or having a spiritual life.

What social constructionist thinking means for working effectively with young children is that it encourages us to challenge our own 'givens' in thinking about children and their families. Suspending our own assumptions may provide insight into understanding what meanings specific behaviours might have for someone else's reality (Billington 2000; Laws and Davies 2000).

How children and families are discussed among the staff in your centre will be a way of 'constructing' how you perceive them (Roffey *et al.* 2000c). If everyone talks about a child as 'aggressive' then behaviours will be interpreted as such. This impacts both on responses to the child and on conversations with parents. 'Co-constructing' reality means careful listening and observation to discover what a behaviour means (Roffey 2002).

 CASE STUDY

Jessie was always in trouble in the playground for screaming, pushing and kicking other children. A close observation showed that children were excluding her from games and that her behaviour was a distressed reaction. Staff had seen only one side of the interaction and Jessie was being blamed. The problem was therefore self perpetuating and needed adult intervention so that Jessie could be included.

Social constructionist theory also helps construct alternative realities for children by offering them opportunities to develop different stories to make sense of the world. Narrative therapy, which is based in social constructionist thinking, focuses on the relationship that a person has with a problem rather than seeing the person as the problem. Some early years teachers do this naturally: *Well, Mr Grumpy seems to have got hold of you this morning, Michael. Is he stopping you enjoying yourself?*

Social learning theory

This theory originating with Alfred Bandura (1971) says that all behaviour is learnt, and takes account of the many factors involved in this learning. Early years teachers are well placed to adopt this theory as it replicates much of what they will have in place for learning within the academic curriculum.

Social learning theory places a strong emphasis on modelling. Children copy what they see and hear. This is vitally important in thinking about behaviour. Those tiny tots whose mouths are full of obscenity are only copying what they have heard. Being outraged at such behaviour is out of place. Children need to be told each time that these words are not used here in this centre.

Social learning theory also focuses on the need to 'scaffold' learning so that it builds on what someone already knows and helps them make sense of it. It also ensures that targets are within reach so that a child can feel successful and motivated to go further. Vygotsky (1978) calls this the 'zone of proximal development' sometimes referred to as 'working in the tomorrow of the child'. It involves identifying emergent behaviours (what the child can do with help) in order to scaffold learning towards independence (what a child can do without help).

Learning theory also helps us to understand that there are different levels of learning and if we target teaching at the appropriate level the child will be more successful:

▶ The first step is 'Acquisition' – learning something new for the first time. This requires interactive teaching – being shown and helped to understand.

▶ Next comes 'Rehearsal' – this requires opportunities to practise the new skill – usually in structured settings with constructive feedback.

▶ 'Adaptation' is where the skill is applied in a new situation.

▶ 'Generalization' is the ability to be flexible and adaptive with the skill across a range of situations.

▶ 'Fluency' is the ability to apply the skill in all relevant situations without having to think too hard about it.

For adults you can see how this would apply to learning a new language – or learning to drive, something they have probably chosen to do. Think for a moment about a child learning a new social skill – perhaps to take turns in a group situation. Not only might it be quite a challenging process that takes some time to achieve, but the teacher also needs to encourage the motivation to want to learn these skills. This will be based in relationship and natural reward – such as enjoyment in the game.

Behaviourist theory

This theory focuses entirely on what is observable. It does not take account of what the child thinks or feels, except to identify what provides reinforcement for different behaviours. The theory says that behaviour only occurs in a context and what comes before and after the behaviour can either encourage or discourage it. If, for instance, everyone laughs when a child pours water on his head and the child finds this attention delightful, he is likely to repeat it. If all he gets is cold and wet the behaviour is less likely to occur!

We know that human beings and their motivations are much more complex than this – the high level of recidivism after the negative reinforcement of imprisonment is proof that punishment alone does not change behaviour. If children only behave in pro-social ways for a promised extrinsic reward or because of feared punishment then they will not develop moral codes for themselves (see Chapter 2).

Some behaviourist approaches, however, do have some value as management strategies and as such are included here. The strategy based on behaviourist theory is often referred to as the ABC model:

A = Antecedents: what happens within the context prior to the observable behaviour.
B = Behaviour: describes what actually happens in observable terms.
C = Consequences: what happens immediately afterwards.

The aim is to change either the antecedents or the consequences in order to change the behaviour.

It is possible to use a solution-focused ABC model to identify ways forward for the child rather than focus on the problem, i.e. what is happening when a wanted behaviour is occurring rather than when a problem behaviour is happening (Roffey 2004a).

DIFFERENCES BETWEEN CHILDREN

All practitioners instinctively know that children are different but do not always take into account the wide diversity this might mean and how it impacts on the ease or difficulty with which children settle. Children arriving at an early years centre bring an understanding of themselves and the world based on the many experiences and interactions they have already had. This includes anticipated responses if they explore, ask questions, make demands and so on. Some children have

CASE STUDY

Oscar often bothers other children by poking or pushing them. The wanted behaviour is that he keeps his hands to himself. Most of the time he is able to do this, but the unwanted behaviour increases towards the end of the session.

Antecedent for wanted behaviour: Oscar is less likely to bother others when he is fully occupied.

Behaviour: Oscar is involved in creative, constructive activity.

Consequence: Oscar is talking to himself and whoever is nearby about what he is doing. The teacher is occasionally remarking on his achievements.

Plan

Antecedent: When Oscar is not occupied he will be given something to do such as a drawing or puzzle.

Consequence: Oscar will be regularly commended for his ability to interact 'nicely' with other children.

Observations indicated that Oscar was less likely to bother other children at the beginning of the day. It was possible that being more tired or hungry towards lunchtime was having a negative impact. This was also true, however, of others. Rather than single out Oscar it was decided that this latter part of the morning was a good time to carry out a circle-time activity with everyone. Children were also given the opportunity to have a second piece of fruit to help 'keep them going' until lunchtime.

had things explained while others are reprimanded for anything and everything. Children also learn which behaviours result in high levels of attention from caregivers. Some rarely receive positive attention for wanted behaviours and as a consequence may not know what is wanted from the adults in the centre and are relying on guesswork.

Children grow up in families where different things are valued and/ or important. For some regular prayer is routine, in others anxious conversations about money happen on a daily basis. For some parents looking 'nice' is more important than children having fun in messy activities while other families consider cleanliness a low priority. Many families have an established routine for when and how certain things happen, such as mealtimes and bedtimes. In others things happen fairly haphazardly. Some children learn that there is a beginning, middle and end to many activities, others have minimal experience of this.

There are children with access to a wealth of toys and play materials. Some have adults play with them and are encouraged to explore, be creative and extend their worlds. They may get taken on outings and holidays and given opportunities to experience many things. Children who live in families where books are all around and a bedtime story part of the routine will already have a 'concept of print' and an idea that books are full of great possibilities. Other children spend a good deal of time in front of the television while parents work or are busy elsewhere. Some have little access to either the written word or mediated play experiences. There are families who do not see play as a central development activity for children and expect that when they 'go to school', even though they are only three, they will sit and do formal activities aimed at meeting more academic goals. The value of play in learning and the rationale for pre-school activities may need to be explained to parents.

Secure children have a sense of being special within their family. They are wanted, loved and valued. As we know, this is not true of all. By the time they come to pre-school some children will have got the message that they are a nuisance. Others will be scared of making mistakes, getting things wrong or speaking up.

Some children have been denied nothing. Parents may give the impression they can do no wrong and give in to whatever demands they make. Adults may not have the energy or will to set any clear boundaries. Occasionally, children are encouraged to be highly dependent and stay the 'baby' of the family. These groups of children will also have a hard time realizing that expectations in the centre are different.

For those in stable and loving families, adults are people who look after you and help you – they provide safety, affection and nurturance. Less fortunate children may be fearful of adults for their violent, cold or erratic behaviour. These children may be unable to explore their environment with ease because they have been given messages that are not conducive to curiosity.

10

Children come into pre-school with a wide range of skills and levels of development. These include comprehension, self-help skills, communication skills, and ability to focus, pay attention and complete something. Levels of development impact on learning but also on social understanding and behaviour, emotional regulation and repertoires for expression. Children also arrive with different personalities. It is the subtle and complex interactions between the predispositions and potential that the child brings and the environments in which they spend their time which determine outcomes for self-esteem, achievement and behaviour.

All pre-school children, however, bring with them a developmental level which is still highly egocentric. They are able to tune into others but will understand them only in terms of what they know about themselves. Taking account of that egocentricity is essential if we are to help children move into the stage of increased perspective taking and more pro-social behaviour.

WHAT CHILDREN BRING WITH THEM

► experiences of interactions

► an understanding of what will happen if . . .

► knowledge of how best to get attention

► ideas of what is and isn't important

► experiences of play and exploring

► a developing self-image

► views of themselves within their family

► varying skills of communication

► feelings of fear or security

► different levels of development and skill acquisition

► a developmental level which is basically egocentric

► messages about learning – making them excited, eager and curious or fearful and anticipating failure

► their distinct personality and characteristics.

EARLY INTERVENTION FOR BEHAVIOUR

Differences between children are largely associated with the varied experiences they have had in their early years. Many children settle well into the pre-school setting. They are confident, responsive and outgoing. These may be children whose family system mirrors that of the centre. They are also often the children who are easy to warm to. Others are bewildering or just wild! They may have fragmented attention, poor independence, take little notice of others, grab, shove and scream. These children are often more difficult to like but need support, help and guidance even more than the 'good ones'. Often what is required is the good practice you provide for all children, just more specific, targeted or simply more of it! Good practice in early years education is good practice for *all* children.

Whether they are able, energetic but lacking self-control or distressed and 'hard to manage', all children require encouragement and help to understand what is expected of them. They need to know what is involved in getting along with other children so that they can begin to enjoy the benefits of collaborative play. They need to learn that they will get acknowledgement for behaving in pro-social ways and have success experiences structured for them so they begin to develop a self-concept of being able. In general they need to think of themselves more positively. Demands on children need to be at an appropriate level for their current learning and development. This includes their emotional competence and their communication skills.

It also matters that children learn that although some of their behaviour is unwanted, they are important. When they have experiences of 'belonging' they will have increased motivation and willingness to cooperate. They may need to learn to trust others as kind, 'safe', 'fair' and consistent – that adults will follow through with what they say. Children also need to have some control over what happens to them and be given options to choose.

In summary, children who are more difficult to manage are likely to need the following:

▶ encouragement to think of themselves positively;
▶ to develop a concept of themselves as able to learn and be successful;
▶ help in understanding what is expected of them;
▶ to be taught skills to help them get along with others;

- ► to learn to get attention by positive behaviours;
- ► to learn to trust others as kind, 'safe', 'fair' and consistent;
- ► to learn that they matter, they are important and they belong;
- ► to have some control over what happens to them;
- ► acceptance of their emotions and help to express these safely;
- ► opportunities to develop and positively display strengths and qualities.

CONCLUSION

Evidence suggests that where children do not have the foundations to develop social and emotional competencies they are at risk of escalating academic and behavioural problems. In the worse scenarios such individuals eventually drop out of school with all the implications of social exclusion. What happens in these early stages, in the child's first placement, is therefore crucial. This knowledge brings with it an immense responsibility, but an equally significant privilege. Good practice in an early years setting may very well make a difference for the rest of a child's life. Early years educators have a vital role in creating the society of tomorrow. The rest of this book details what practitioners might do that will make that difference and what they might need to help them do it.

Chapter 2

Learning to be 'good'

What do young children know of right and wrong? What values do we want them to have? What should we expect from children in the early years? What is developmentally appropriate? What do we want from children in different contexts? What do they need to develop empathy and positive relationships with others? How can we help them learn?

Being 'good' is a slippery term. We hear babies being described as 'good' when they sleep all the time and 'difficult' when they are crying with colic. What we are really referring to is how easy their behaviour is for their caregivers. The curious one-year-old who wants to push buttons, pull earrings and throw things on the floor to see what happens can be regarded as 'bright and lively' by one mother but as 'demanding' or 'naughty' by another. By the time these children enter early years settings much of their understanding of what is right and wrong will have been established by how significant caregivers have responded to them. Where one child has experienced toleration of testing out without many boundaries and another has had a parent with no patience at all then each has different things to learn in the early years setting: the first that other people matter and the second that he does.

In the past in Western society being 'good' entailed children being 'seen and not heard'. Now it often means 'doing as you're told' but also 'standing up for yourself'. In many cultures approval is linked with conformity to family and community expectations and individuality is conceptualized as selfishness. The focus on individual achievement in Western societies, where value is often put on being 'better' and having more than others, is less conducive to the development of pro-social attitudes and behaviour (Thompson and Gullone 2003).

CASE STUDY

Tara was in the park with her three-year-old daughter. One of the swings was broken; in the other a small boy was being pushed by his mother. Tara waited patiently while the boy had his turn – which went on and on. After about five minutes Tara politely asked the mother when her little girl could have a go. The mother ignored her and after a while Tara asked again. The mother then turned to her and said 'I will be here for as long as I like'.

When the boy goes to an early years centre he will not understand that others have rights and he has responsibilities because this has not been modelled to him. He may also think he can have whatever he wants when he wants it. This does not bode well for his healthy development, his social relationships with peers or the promotion of empathy in society.

Children are born egocentric for their own survival; they need to grow into being cooperative for the survival of the species! Healthy development in the early years is marked by a 'decentralization' process by which children increasingly take the perspectives of others and learn ways of relating that makes group activity possible. Children who are not taught to take others into consideration do not develop knowledge and skills that enable them to have strong and healthy relationships. We can see the outcomes of this in increased family and community breakdown and deteriorating mental health in the Western world.

Louise Porter (1997) suggests that we need to teach children to be considerate and for that they have to develop four skills:

▶   personal accountability – an autonomous understanding of right from wrong – in the absence of anyone telling them;
▶   responsibility for self and the ability to manage emotions;
▶   the capacity to cooperate with others;
▶   a sense of personal agency – to know they can make a difference for themselves and for others, make decisions that affect them and act on their own sense of right and wrong.

So how do children develop this understanding of right and wrong – of what it means to be 'good'? How do they learn what it means to be 'considerate' so that it eventually becomes their way of being and of choice?

APPROACHES THAT DO NOT WORK IN THE LONGER TERM

Although children need to know what counts as unacceptable behaviour, 'strong discipline' in which children learn to be obedient to an external control is not in the children's best interests and in some circumstances may even be dangerous. Authoritarian approaches, which 'make' children behave in certain ways by routinely using threat and punishment, promote initial fear, later anger and invariably resentment. They also model aggression as a way of getting what you want.

Children who are routinely smacked are much more likely to hit others as they have learnt from significant adults that this is acceptable. Although corporal punishment can be seen to have an effective short-term impact, punitive approaches don't work well overall and certainly not in the longer term where they can have a damaging effect on mental health. This is especially true when there is no warm relationship to back up the 'discipline' (Turner and Muller 2004).

Children who are regularly punished may also be overwhelmed with fear and not able to think clearly enough to internalize moral rules. Pupils who are simply punished for disobedience are more likely to behave in uncontrolled ways when the 'big stick' is no longer held over them. You can see this in classes in both primary and high schools where there is a continual battle between students and teachers for who has 'control'. The effort to keep a tighter and tighter rein on classes is wearing for teachers, some of whom give up the profession altogether (Stoel and Thant 2002).

APPROACHES THAT DO WORK

Research by Baumrind (1971) into parenting styles and developed since by many others (e.g. Mapinga *et al.* 2002) has shown clearly which adult–child interactions are most conducive to the development of pro-social functioning and positive mental health outcomes. The research is indisputable. The authoritative style facilitates learning pro-social behaviours and the relationships that significant adults have with children is crucial. As authoritative and authoritarian are such similar words a clearer term for this optimal style of interaction is 'facilitative'.

16

Facilitative parenting styles are where the parent/child relationship is distinguished not only by warmth and affection but also clear consistent expectations and boundaries. Children know what is acceptable behaviour and do not 'get away' with behaviour that is unacceptable. They are, however, encouraged to think through their actions rather than simply being told to obey an external authority. Communication between adults and children involves listening as well as talking and there are frameworks in place for reflection and collaboration. Over time this provides for the development of an internal control. Children learn to behave in socially responsible ways because they appreciate the harmful consequences to themselves and others if they do not. They also have a vested interest in maintaining the relationships within which they are learning 'how to behave'.

There is evidence that warm, democratic parental styles, where families focus on developmental needs, provide choices and value close relationships, strengthen intrinsic values such as self development and autonomy, affiliation and community feeling (Kasser *et al.* 2002). When children experience cold, controlling and rejecting environments, this appears to foster values where obtaining external rewards are seen as most desirable. This is not beneficial for relationships or mental health.

There are several aspects to the facilitative approach:

- ▶ warmth towards and acceptance of the child;
- ▶ clear boundaries for behaviour, applied consistently but flexibly;
- ▶ developmentally appropriate expectations;
- ▶ structured, supported and developmentally appropriate opportunities to solve problems;
- ▶ the provision of appropriate role models;
- ▶ positive feedback by significant adults;
- ▶ adults who are prepared to listen as well as tell;
- ▶ succinct rationales for behaviour that promote fairness and belonging.

For the most part there is neither the time nor the need in early years settings to provide lengthy explanations about why children should behave in certain ways. A succinct rationale, however, is valuable:

- ▶ *Please clear up now so that we can be ready for going outside.*
- ▶ *It is now Darren's turn — you have had yours.*

Induction

Research shows (Kochanska 1991) that whereas strongly punitive approaches decrease feelings of guilt in harming others, the use of inductive reasoning promotes more pro-social or altruistic behaviour (Hoffman 1988). This points out the effects of children's behaviour on others, gives children information about how to behave and fosters empathy:

> ▶ *Pulling Kirsty's hair hurt her. You would not like it if someone hurt you like that.*
>
> ▶ *Telling Alex that you don't like him makes him very sad. Perhaps it would make you sad if someone said that to you?*

Negotiation

Children are never too young to have their opinions considered about matters that affect them (Miller 1996). Even those who have limited language skills can make their choices known. Young children who are listened to and whose views are taken into account will feel valued and have a sense of agency. This is likely to result in them being able to take more responsibility for their actions and the internalization of pro-social moral codes. This does not mean that everything a child wants will be agreed and provided. Sometimes choices will be limited and sometimes they will be refused. But children who are given agency may very well use that in pro-social ways and experience the positives of caring behaviour.

 CASE STUDY

Three-year-old Caitlin was fed up with walking and wanted to be carried. When her Dad, Jon, tried to persuade her to go further she began to stamp and scream. Jon offered Caitlin a choice. 'If I carried you as far as that tree would you try to walk from there?' Caitlin stopped screaming and agreed. She was also happy to walk again when they got to the tree.

Approaches which give children choice also facilitate a more peaceful ethos within an educational setting and are more beneficial to everyone (Hromek 2004).

Natural consequences

This is different from consequences imposed for unacceptable behaviour. It is the explanation of what will naturally occur as a result of actions: *Throwing water on the floor makes it slippery. Someone may get hurt. If you want to play with the water it must stay in the sink.* It is even better if children are encouraged to think about consequences themselves.

Principles for behaviour

In early years settings practitioners need to agree principles for their definitions of 'good' behaviour. Which behaviours are important for the benefit of the child and the pre-school community and what is simply a question of social order? Policies that are developed in tandem with discussions about values have a stronger foundation and more clarity in implementation.

Basic values for an early years centre might be:

▶ everyone is included;
▶ everyone is valued;
▶ everyone is treated fairly;
▶ we look out for each other;
▶ we help each other;
▶ we are kind to each other;
▶ we listen to each other.

If this is what we want for our children, this is what we need to show them. By far the most powerful learning tool is observation and imitation. Children will copy the interactions they have seen, the words they have heard and the expression of emotions they have experienced. Early years professionals have the opportunity to demonstrate a model that may provide an alternative to others the children have known.

Understanding of right and wrong

It may seem obvious, but people do sometimes forget that children's understanding of what is good and bad, right and wrong, acceptable or not is not innate. Little children cannot be expected to automatically know what is considered to be 'correct' behaviour and making assumptions that they 'ought' to is not helpful. It is easy to forget that pre-schoolers are at this highly egocentric stage of development – they are

19

only just learning to take the perspective of others and need help to do this.

Children's academic learning is facilitated by teaching, reminding, and encouragement. We do not punish mistakes but see them as a natural part of the process. The same principles need to apply to learning about behaviour.

Like learning to walk and talk, 'moral' development is an incremental process but unlike learning to walk and talk the path this takes is almost entirely dependent on context. A child who grows up in one environment will have a different understanding of what is expected of her than someone who grows up in another. Small children learn quickly what is important to their caregivers, both in terms of the way these people themselves act and in terms of responses to their own behaviour. Developing notions of right and wrong, care and justice, stem from this. By two years toddlers will be indicating quite clearly what is likely to bring disapproval or approval by their caregivers. Because different families have different expectations it is unsurprising that many children come into early years provision with a set of beliefs, values and judgements that are in conflict with those within the setting.

 CASE STUDY

Xenia comes with her parents to a rather nice lunch party. Xenia is three and an only, much loved child. After lunch everyone is sitting around having coffee. Xenia decides to dance – she takes centre stage and for the best part of 30 minutes, twirls and twists, interrupting conversations, treading on toes and bumping into hands holding coffee cups. It is a miracle nothing is spilt. Xenia is doing nothing 'wrong' but by mid-afternoon several people are muttering beneath their breath about her 'uncontrolled precocious behaviour'. Her parents are oblivious – she has delighted them with her antics.

Children do not always understand why they get into trouble – it can be very confusing sorting out what pleases the grown ups and what upsets them – especially when it seems to be almost the same thing.

CASE STUDY

Four-year-old Lucas had just learnt how to use scissors and had spent the morning cutting pictures from magazines. Everyone had been very pleased with him. They were less pleased when he used his new-found skills on the heads of the garden flowers.

Developmental goals

Early years practitioners do not need to be told that the capacity for pre-schoolers to learn is greater than at any other time in their lives. Young children are supposed to be curious, into everything, having a go, seeing what happens, trying things out, being little scientists and creators. They have a drive towards independence and are supposed to want to do things for themselves! Learning, independence, communication and experimentation are fundamental goals for pre-school children, just as much as pro-social behaviour.

Our role as early years educators is to nurture that curiosity, mediate learning and scaffold growing independence. When you are in the thrall of a timetable and curriculum expectations, however, it may be tempting to structure for conformity where individual strengths and interests take second place to adult needs and goals. 'Being good' is only one goal among the other developmentally appropriate ones of:

▶ 'being interested and curious' (motivation);
▶ 'challenging boundaries' (innovation and identity);
▶ 'exploring the unknown' (experiential learning and understanding);
▶ 'trying out possibilities' (imagination and creativity);
▶ 'doing it myself' (independence).

Some of these goals will at times seem to be in conflict with 'being good'. Children may 'get into trouble' for behaving in ways which they are supposed to do at this age. Adults need to take into account the developmental stage children are at and what is actually possible for them. If small children are told to do something and their curiosity distracts them onto something else this reflects the inability to hold several thoughts in their heads rather than being disobedient. A three-year-old whose struggle for

21

independence means they challenge adult authority is not being 'disrespectful', they are doing what 'comes naturally'. It requires subtle and complex skills of early years practitioners to ensure that they honour children's development while fostering cooperation so that the various goals within the centre remain congruent.

As a young teacher of reception class (kindergarten) children, I once found myself saying with exasperation at the end of a long and tiring day 'you are all behaving like a bunch of five-year-olds!' Thirty little faces looked at me with astonishment – and one small voice from the back piped up 'I'm only four'. When you spend all your time working in early years settings it is easy to forget just how little these children are and that sometimes they are just 'being kids'. It is worth considering whether or not it is necessary to intervene in any given situation. There is only so much time and energy that you can expend. If behaviour is developmentally appropriate and not hurting anyone – even if it is irritating – what is the minimal response possible? If you can't ignore it altogether, perhaps just a comment might be all that is needed.

Rough and tumble play is a good example of this. Watching a litter of kittens or puppies demonstrates that all young animals jump on each other and chase each other around. Do not assume that children are having a fight that has to be stopped unless it is clear that the interaction is very unequal and someone is getting hurt.

MORAL DEVELOPMENT THEORIES

There are several theories about moral understanding and behaviour and how this develops. Kohlberg (1984) and Piaget (1965) say pre-school-aged children are at the stage of moral development in which they either:

▶ do as they are told by those in authority or risk getting into trouble; or

▶ do what will win the approval of significant people.

According to this theory children have little understanding about intention and determine how 'bad' something is with the outcome. This means that a child who accidentally broke six cups might be seen to be in more trouble than the child who deliberately smashed just one. Piaget is now considered to have underestimated children's abilities, especially when they are exposed to the influence of mediation and discussion. Adults who talk with children about intention and accidents help them see that some things that happen are not deliberate. This may not ease the pain of a bruised knee when someone has knocked a child down by not looking where they were going – but it may soothe a bruised sense of justice.

The same might be applied to the distributive justice theory. Pre-school children want everything to be shared out fairly and equally but discussions may introduce an early understanding that different needs may require different responses.

Peer interactions in early years settings are important as they present the developing child with different views that require negotiation. According to Selman's theory (1980) of 'perspective taking' children between the ages of three and six recognize differences between them-selves and others but often confuse this. Helping children 'tune' into others by reference to themselves is therefore more likely to be effec-tive in promoting empathy.

Jimmy is upset today because someone stole his new bike. Have you lost something very important? Can you remember how you felt? Did anything help you feel better?

In her theory on moral development Carol Gilligan emphasizes the 'ethic of care' over the concept of justice (Gilligan and Wiggins 1988). She takes the view that 'justice' is male-dominated moral reasoning and does not give sufficient credence to the importance of care and respon-siveness in moral values. In early years settings this means giving both boys and girls opportunities to think about what is 'kind' as well as what is 'fair'.

Research and theories on moral development have different emphases but all are useful in raising awareness about what it means for young children in learning about 'being good':

▶ Children will sometimes be surprised when they get into trouble.
▶ They cannot always predict the response to their actions.
▶ They may be more concerned with outcome than with motivation and intent.
▶ They believe they are not liked or loved when an adult is cross with them.
▶ Children's developmental goals and abilities may be in conflict with adult demands for 'good behaviour'.

► Discussion about moral issues helps children learn about others and think through social dilemmas.
► Children need opportunities for negotiation in real life situations.

Violent play themes

There is some debate about the level of 'violent' play that some young children indulge in. Should we be worried – and should we stop it? In her book on the subject Penny Holland (2003) acknowledges the complexity of the subject and says that although there is some evidence (Dunn and Hughes 2001) of connections between violent play at four and anti-social behaviour at six, this does not clarify mediation factors. She considers that zero tolerance of such play may inhibit the opportunity for talking about conflict, a skill that is increasingly necessary in today's violent world. Actively engaging with the issues may help children to learn about consequences and alternatives. This is very different from allowing such play free rein and fits in with what the moral development theorists tell us about 'learning to be good'.

The development of empathy

As children's ability to 'decentralize' takes place they are increasingly able to take on board the perspective of others. Pre-schoolers, especially those with sufficient language skills, can find ways to show comfort and concern. Experiences and parental models are powerful influences and empathic behaviour is fostered by the approaches and actions taken by significant people. These mirror the principles of facilitative parenting given earlier, especially the provision of models for empathic care-giving and clarity and conviction of expectation.

Children who have a pro-social and confident temperament and are able to regulate their own emotions are also likely to be more empathic (Eisenberg *et al.* 1996). See Chapter 4 for ways to develop confidence and emotional regulation.

SUMMARY: HOW DO CHILDREN LEARN TO BE 'GOOD'?

► Having warm, supportive 'significant' relationships.
► Knowing what 'being good' means.

▶ Being shown by significant people.

▶ Finding 'good' behaviour rewarding – pleasing significant people matters.

▶ If being 'good' does not conflict with developmental needs.

▶ Having enough choice and control to maximize eventual internalization.

▶ Developmentally appropriate guidance to develop 'perspective taking' and tune into others.

▶ Being given pro-social attributions.

▶ Mediation and discussion to problem-solve real-life situations.

▶ Clarification of the consequences for inconsiderate or otherwise unacceptable behaviour.

And, for the record, the following is less likely to work:

▶ Shouting (children hear the sound rather than the instruction).

▶ Nagging (children switch off – we all do!).

▶ A focus on punishment (provides unhelpful models and does not give guidance).

▶ Being told what *not* to do all the time (no clear direction about what to do).

▶ Inconsistent expectations.

▶ Being made to feel incompetent (we all try to live up to expectations).

▶ Being compared with others (sets up resentment).

▶ Having love withdrawn (leads to anxiety rather than internalization of values).

Chapter 3

Behaviour begins with a 'C'

It just so happens that most of the fundamental principles of establishing and maintaining pro-social behaviour begin with a 'C'. This helps in remembering what they are! The same basics apply at all ages but are especially important in the early years. The following guidelines are for ALL children – both those who are easy to manage and those who are more challenging. The more specific interventions discussed in other chapters are not replacements for what is covered here. These principles should already be in place. This chapter is divided into three parts. The first shows how to establish positive behaviour, the next section covers what you might do in the first instance when individual behaviour is unacceptable and the third section focuses on aspects of the bigger picture in your setting.

Cooperation is part of the human condition. We need to get along with others for our mutual survival. Most of us, young and old, want to work and play together! In order to actively demonstrate the cooperative and pro-social behaviour required in pre-school, however, children need to:

- ▶ know exactly what is required;
- ▶ be able to do it;
- ▶ not be too tired, hungry, cold or anxious;
- ▶ feel good about doing it;
- ▶ not find it a threat;
- ▶ feel supported to be successful.

The following gives more detail on thinking about and constructing situations in which positive behaviours can be best established.

I: ESTABLISHING PRO-SOCIAL BEHAVIOUR

Context

Behaviour only has meaning within the context in which it occurs. What might be perfectly acceptable in one situation may not be in another. The pre-school setting is a particular kind of context; different from others the child may have been in. Some children are on a very steep learning curve and need scaffolding to be successful.

The early years setting either can be set up to reduce behavioural difficulties or can exacerbate them. The following prevents unnecessary conflict:

- ▶ being clear about who has what when;
- ▶ having enough to go round;
- ▶ putting boundaries around activities e.g. paint stays in this area so it can't spoil the books and toys;
- ▶ giving enough space for physical activities so participating children don't crash into each other;
- ▶ showing children how to use equipment and giving them supervised practice;
- ▶ regularly encouraging and reminding children to 'use your words' to say what they need, ask questions, express hurt. Some children may need help with this (see Chapter 5);
- ▶ sequencing – this happens, then that. Giving notice of changes;
- ▶ grouping – to avoid everyone clamouring to do the same thing at once;
- ▶ regularly mixing up groups so that in time everyone gets to play and work with everyone else.

Clarity about expectations

Before we can communicate to the children how we want them to behave we need to be clear about this ourselves. This might sound obvious but in practice we do not always sort out what is important and what is less so.

It is likely that you will have some 'rules' for children but you will also have 'routines'. Some rules are related to values that you wish to instil in the children and will be central to the ethos in your centre. Many will be about how people relate to each other. Examples of rules might be:

▶ We are kind to each other.
▶ We take turns.

When children are behaving in ways that are unacceptable referring to 'what happens here' reinforces the contextual element which is non-judgemental. For example, to the child who has just used a string of expletives towards a peer you can say: *We are kind to each other here and speaking like that is unkind. We do not use those words here.*

Routines are about how the centre is managed and may include such rules as:

▶ We all tidy up at the end of the morning.
▶ We wash our hands before having our snack.

Children need reminders before reprimands. Ask a child if she knows what she is supposed to do. If she does not then tell her and ask her to repeat this to you.

Clear, positive communication

Experienced early years practitioners are now aware that it is more useful to tell children *what* to do rather than what *not* to do. Both individuals and groups are more likely to comply if you tell them what it is you want rather than just stopping what they are doing.

For example, say:

Speak in a voice I can hear, instead of *Stop screaming at me.*

Wait behind Joe for your turn, instead of *Don't push in.*

Hyacinth, turn round and look at me, instead of *Hyacinth, leave Paula alone.*

Any rules in the centre need to be positively phrased and few in number. It is even better if children are part of the establishment of these rules so that they not only remember what they are — but why they are there. Words like 'kind' and 'friendly' need to have much discussion and illustration.

Many small children do not have well-established verbal skills. They may not understand what they hear you say (see Chapter 5). Expectations therefore need to be communicated in many ways:

CASE STUDY

Focus on Friendship: The teachers had put a big 'friendship tree' on one wall and the children were 'growing' this by putting leaves on the tree. On each leaf was written the name of the child or children who had acted in a particularly friendly way and what it was they had done. 'Vikram helped Adnan find his lost shoe', 'Alice and Kerrie asked Nora to play with them.' Each leaf was placed on the tree with great ceremony at the end of each day. The children were also given badges when staff 'caught' them being friendly. The badges simply said 'I was a good friend today' but the children were able to tell you exactly what they had done to win their badge.

► demonstrating and modelling: showing what is expected;
► giving children chances to copy and practise *how* to carry out routines;
► visual support: pictures, diagrams, labels, etc.;
► physical guidance: doing things together, gesture, facial expression and even miming.

It is not only the children who need to know what is expected. Parents and carers benefit from having clear and accessible information about what happens in the centre. It is also helpful if they are given explanations about why these things are considered important. This will help as well in discussions about difficulties (see Chapter 7).

Concise communication

Kind, gentle adults often want to explain to children why they should behave in certain ways. They go into a detailed rationale and the bemused children stand and nod when asked 'do you understand?' When an individual goes and does the precise opposite the kindly adult is surprised and may be cross that the child has 'taken no notice'. This can set up a negative spiral. Experienced early years practitioners know that simple language and short sentences are much more effective. There are several reasons for this:

▶ small children can only understand and remember a few separate pieces of information at any one time;

▶ their attention span is short;

▶ they may not understand all the words you use;

▶ they may not be tuned into sequential understanding very well so have fewer strategies for remembering;

▶ a high proportion of young children have conductive hearing loss, especially when they have a cold, and this impacts on their comprehension and language development;

▶ the more able children may find this an ideal place to secure your presence and attention and keep you engaged.

Keep it short!

Consistency

Consistency is important in several ways:

▶ Consistency of expectations – that people do not change what they want from children at whim.

▶ Consistency of response – so children know what will happen in response to what they are saying, doing and not doing.

▶ Consistency of words and actions – telling a child that her behaviour is unacceptable while laughing or giving other positive messages will reinforce the behaviour, whatever words you say.

Children need to know where they stand. Managing different expectations in two different places is one thing and some children manage this better than others – but getting into trouble for something one minute and getting rewarded for it the next by the same person is confusing. Where there is little or no consistency children will learn:

▶ how they behave does not really matter;

▶ adults are unreliable and do not always do what they say;

▶ difficult behaviour sometimes brings rewards.

As the case study on p. 31 shows, some children need help to learn that adults in the early years centre mean what they say and will follow through. This learning will not happen overnight. If Chloe continually

CASE STUDY

Two-year-old Chloe asked for sweets in the supermarket queue. Her mother, Stella, said 'No'. Chloe started to whine and tug at her mother's coat. Stella got more and more cross with her and shouted 'I said no!' Her cries got louder and more tearful. When they got to the checkout Stella had had enough, bought the sweets and gave them to Chloe saying, 'Oh, here you are then, now stop making such a fuss.'

Chloe will have learnt that her whining works in getting her what she wants. So long as she keeps it up her mother will give in. If Stella tries to be strong and stick to her words Chloe will begin by getting louder and more strident in her demands. Stella will have a much harder time managing her behaviour in the future.

gets into trouble and is blamed for this whining behaviour, it will take longer to change than if it is seen as a learning target and her small successes in getting there acknowledged.

Consistency, however, does not mean rigidity. There are times when it may be inappropriate to stringently apply 'the rules' because this does not meet individual needs or a particular situation. If you do apply exceptions on occasions ensure that everyone knows that this is what you are doing and why.

Catch the child being 'good'

One of the best ways of getting children to understand what it is that you want from them (and do more of it!) is to give maximum attention to desired behaviour and minimal attention to unwanted behaviour. Rather than just wait to catch them out when they are 'misbehaving' and jump in with a 'don't', it is far more effective to comment on what they are doing well. This has several outcomes:

▶ it makes the child feel good about complying rather than upset about being 'told off';
▶ it reinforces positive relationships – the keystone of strategy success;

CASE STUDY

Ahmet is a bright, knowledgeable four-year-old. He settled well into the early years centre and has good concentration for self-chosen tasks. It soon became clear, however, that Ahmet became angry if not allowed to have his own way, e.g. refusing to join in with tidying up and not being willing to share with other children. Further observation and discussion revealed no apparent developmental, medical, social or family issues.

Following a discussion at a special needs consultation group and visit from an early years advisory teacher the following strategies were suggested:

▶ Records of Ahmet's 'outbursts' indicated that these were most likely to happen after the first hour of the morning. It appeared that Ahmet was finding it very difficult to leave the activity he was engaged in for drinks/circle time. It was suggested that drinks be freely available throughout the session and circle time changed to a shorter session at the beginning.

▶ Observations revealed that Ahmet had different responses from different staff members when he refused to do something. Some staff members would insist he complied with a request, others would allow him to refuse. It was suggested that a consistent strategy be agreed to be followed by all members of staff. It was decided that all adults would insist that Ahmet comply with a request, e.g. at tidy-up time he would be prompted to do some tidying up, or at circle time he would be expected to come and sit down for at least some of the session.

▶ Finally, it was agreed that Ahmet would have the following target on his individual education plan: 'Ahmet will join in a simple turn-taking game with one other child, adult mediating' and that his key worker would make sure he included Ahmet in such a game at least once every session.

At a review after six weeks, staff reported that Ahmet was much happier in the setting, that he was complying with most adult requests and no longer having angry outbursts.

▶ it has a 'ripple' effect on others nearby who are more likely to take notice, Canter (1992) calls this 'proximity praise';

▶ it gives greater clarity to what is expected.

It is important that children are told *Good girl for* . . . or *Thank you for* . . . rather than simply told *Good*. In addition to words a smile or thumbs up or 'hey wow' can have dramatic and positive impact.

Many children, especially those who are struggling to comply with learning behavioural expectations, respond well to tangible, graphic and 'larger than life' feedback. This can be provided by the following:

▶ stickers on books and on arms;

▶ print stamps (as above but cheaper);

▶ badges;

▶ stars on a star chart;

▶ group applause;

▶ certificates to take home;

▶ being asked to show others what to do;

▶ marbles in the jar (Canter 1992): every time a child or group is behaving especially well the teacher says so and drops a marble in a jar, when the jar is full all the children have a special treat. Used wisely this helps to increase children's positive perceptions of themselves and each other.

Many say that you cannot 'ignore' unwanted behaviour, especially if someone is getting hurt or something is being damaged. That is true – you have a responsibility to ensure safety. You can, however, keep your intervention for minor misdemeanours as unrewarding as possible. High-quality attention includes bending down to the child's level, looking them directly in the eye, demonstrating a high degree of emotion and speaking at length. This can be more satisfying than being ignored – even if the purpose is a reprimand. It is better to keep negative interaction short but definite. Children do need to know that their behaviour matters to you so the few words you do say should convey this.

Competencies

Focus on what children *can* do rather than what they are not doing. Help them to feel that they can be successful both with learning and with behaviour. If necessary, comment on the smallest possible step in the right direction and then offer the 'next step' to try. Sometimes it is necessary to set up 'success experiences' that present an achievable target. Once children see they are competent their confidence will increase. It is possible to structure success by giving a child the first step in a task but it may be even better to let them do the last thing to complete a task independently.

Reinforcing emerging social and emotional competencies and telling children that they are *a great help, really listen well, know how to be a friend* impacts on their self-concept and understanding of who they are. If they value the relationship with you they will often try and meet the expectations being given.

Telling children that they can't do something gives them little motivation to try. Giving negative labels reinforces behaviour you don't want.

Confidence

Confidence is a feeling. It is associated with, but not the same as, competence. Confidence needs to be in place if children are to be motivated to continue having a go at things. Confidence can be seriously undermined if making mistakes is not accepted as part of learning.

 CASE STUDY

Harry wanted to have a go on the donkey ride at the fair. He queued up with his parents and in due course was lifted up and placed on the animal. The girl began to lead the donkey around the field. Harry could no longer see his parents and was alarmed at the unfamiliar situation. He began to scream to be let off. His father, furious at the embarrassment this had caused him, shouted at his son saying, 'Don't ever ask to do anything unless you are sure you can do it.' Harry took him at his word and it took patience and determination to encourage Harry to attempt unfamiliar tasks.

One way to promote confidence in children is to let them see that you sometimes make mistakes and learn from these.

Confidence is about believing in yourself. Sometimes children need to attempt things in small stages so that they can build on their successes. If we set targets too high we present children with the fear of failure. We can see this clearly with academic tasks – the same applies to behaviour.

Collaboration with adults

One way of helping children develop confidence is to do things collaboratively. This also provides an emotional cushion if things do not go as well as hoped.

If you ask a child to do something and he refuses or runs off one of the options is to say that you will do it with him. Even if he only manages to do a very small part of the task it is a step in the right direction.

Fostering group cohesion

There are several good reasons for actively addressing groups rather than individuals especially for those who find it more difficult to conform to expectations:

► it is less challenging for children if they are asked as a group to do something rather than making demands of individuals;
► doing things together promotes a sense of fun for children;
► it increases peer pressure to complete something;
► it provides an opportunity for inclusive praise and celebration;
► it is a way of developing a valuable sense of belonging.

Change management

Many adults find it difficult to switch from one situation to another and have to psych themselves up for changes in their lives or for doing something unfamiliar. Yet we do not always prepare children for transitions. It is often at these times that behavioural difficulties emerge. Even though they do not have a clear concept of time it is worth giving children warnings of changes in activity. Most centres already have a routine that leaves the children with no surprises, but some children need more emphatic warnings of change.

CASE STUDY

Three-year-old Martha loved going to play with her friend Josh. They had a great time and she always resisted going home at the end of the afternoon. Her mother, Leonie, was beginning to dread the routine screaming fits. Leonie decided to give Martha notice of when she was going to leave. She did not tell her once but several times so that Martha was well prepared.

'We are going to have tea soon and then we are going home.'

'After we have had tea we must get ready to go.'

'You have nearly finished, so it's nearly home-time.'

'We have all finished tea now. Here is your coat.'

The screaming subsided.

Commentary

Teaching small children 'social skills' is not easily done in formal ways. With the exception of overt modelling, the best way of doing this is to comment on their social interactions to help build pro-social behaviours. Basic social skills emerging at this age are sharing and turn-taking. Without these skills many games and collaborative activities cannot happen. The commentary needs to demonstrate that pro-social behaviours are in the child's interests. They are too young to be altruistic. You may need to monitor the fairness balance in these interactions:

▶ *George, it is Levi's turn to have a go on the bike. You can get back on again later. I will make sure it is fair for everyone.*

▶ *Jacinta, Seema thinks you have a great game. She would love to join in. What would you like her to do?*

▶ *If you snatch the ball every time it comes your way, Timmy, the other children will not want you in their game. What else could you do so you can all play together?*

Comments can also include suggestions for extending creative play. This enhances imagination and cognitive skills. There is more on commentary in Chapter 4.

Construct identities

Children arrive in the early years setting with an emerging self-concept. They will already be thinking of themselves in certain ways and developing an understanding of which labels are to be applied to them – what it means to be a certain gender for instance. Much of what goes on in interaction with others is a way of affirming these constructs.

You can help children create pro-social identities:

► Someone who is often told she is 'really helpful' will try to be so.
► Someone who is praised for being trustworthy for carrying messages will do his best to be the best message-taker he can be.

When children are told they 'can't' do something or that they 'never' behave well they have nothing to live up to except their failure. We need to be very wary of self-fulfilling expectations that reinforce negative behaviour for children.

Choices

Being able to make choices is valuable for everyone. Some small children, however, may be bewildered by completely open-ended choices. When faced with a cornucopia of possibilities being asked 'what do you want?' may give rise to some anxiety about making the 'right' choice. Being given a limited choice, however, puts boundaries around the task and makes it more manageable.

Children also often respond in a more cooperative way if offered a choice. If they are told 'You are going to do this now' it is easy for them to say 'I don't want to'. If they are asked 'would you like to play with the puppets or the Lego?' the option 'neither' is less likely.

Other choices are:

► Sequence choices, e.g. *Would you like to do this first or that first?*, *Would you like to clear up now or after you have finished your painting?*
► Independence choices, e.g. *Are you able to do this by yourself or would you like help?*, *Do you want to take this message by yourself or would you like a friend to go with you?*

37

Giving children a choice of consequences for behaviour is addressed in the next section.

Creative conversations

Telling children what to do and how to behave may help them learn what 'good' means to the adults that they want to please. If, however, they can be encouraged to think through potential conflicts and dilemmas they will discover for themselves ways to address problems. This gives them a better chance of internalizing the values we would like them to develop.

Asking children for possible answers and supporting their 'perspective taking' in a social world will help them learn pro-social and co-operative behaviour 'from the inside' rather than have this continually imposed from without. This scaffolding can make a difference to the development of empathy. There is no doubt that this takes more time but if this is a priority in the early years it promotes a collaborative ethos for the educational environment.

 CASE STUDY

Gavin and Rosie were three-year-old twins. Gavin snatched the toy car that his sister was playing with. Their mother Rachel intervened and put her hand out for the car: 'You can't take that away from Rosie, she was playing with it'; Gavin started to protest and cry that it was his car. Rachel offered him a possible solution: 'Perhaps if you find something that Rosie likes she might swap it for the car.' Gavin went away and came back with a train. Rosie was not impressed and clutched the car to her chest in defiance. Rachel commented: 'That train is what you like to play with – what does Rosie like to play with?' Gavin thought for a moment and his eyes lit up: 'Rosie likes Emily best.' Emily was Rosie's favourite doll. Gavin went off to find her and Rachel helped the situation along by suggesting to Rosie that it would be nice to play with Emily now. Gavin came back with the doll and the swap was made to everyone's satisfaction.

Both Gavin and Rosie learnt that there was the possibility of compromise in the situation. Gavin learnt to take the perspective of his sister and to put himself in her shoes.

This learning can build up to a repertoire of conflict resolution strategies. It is not too young to start.

Congruence

Walking the talk! This is more than consistency of expectations – this means living out our values in ways that do not give mixed messages to children. It is behaving towards children in ways we wish them to behave towards others. They are less likely to learn what it means to be considerate, polite and gentle unless we show them on a daily basis. If we do not yell, make unreasonable demands, nag or use psychological or physical force to 'make' them do what we want then they are less likely to behave in these ways themselves.

SUMMARY OF PART I

Establishing and maintaining pro-social and cooperative behaviour

Context: Bear in mind that behaviour only has meaning in a context. The behaviour you want in your centre may not be what has been required of the child elsewhere. Ensure that the context that you work in limits unnecessary conflict.

Clarity: Children need to learn what is expected of them in different situations. What is it that you want the child to do?

Communication: How do you communicate what it is you want? Turn 'don't' into positive action. Communicating expectations needs to include all staff and families, not only the children.

Be concise: Being brief is more effective than going into detail. It's easy to lose the important message if you say too much.

Catch the child being 'good': it is more effective and facilitates positive relationships. Comment on positive behaviours rather than focus on negative ones.

Consistency: Children learn more quickly if the people around them are consistent in their expectations and responses. Different messages confuse and are open to manipulation.

39

Competencies: Focus on strengths for everyone – what do we all do well?

Confidence: Children will feel more motivated if they know they will not get into trouble or feel bad if they make mistakes.

Collaboration: Doing things together may help.

Change management: Plan for beginnings, endings and transitions between activities. It is here that children are most likely to have difficulty and some forewarning can help.

Commentary: Providing structured opportunities and giving children feedback on their emerging social skills is better than any direct teaching at this stage.

Construct pro-social identities: Children who are told they are helpful are likely to strive to be helpful, those who are told they can't do anything won't try. This is another way of raising awareness of self-fulfilling expectations.

Choices: Children often respond well to being given some control in a situation. Giving limited options often works better; giving time control is often useful. Children who can make choices are more likely to internalize behaviours than if they are just told what to do.

Creative conversations: Be solution focused. Talking and thinking interact in finding ways forward. Ask the child their ideas for solutions.

Congruence: Walk the talk and model the behaviour you want.

II: INITIAL RESPONSES TO UNWANTED BEHAVIOUR

This section deals with what might happen when a child is not doing as required and there is a need to intervene. We focus here on simple non-compliance. For dealing with emotional distress, see Chapters 6 and 7.

Check understanding

Reminders come before reprimands.

Ask the child if he knows what he should be doing:

▶ If it appears that he does not know give clear simple directions and ask if he can do it on his own or whether he needs some help.

▶ If he says he does know you could ask him to tell you what he will do first – and then give him positive and specific feedback for doing it.

For many children this is all that will be necessary.

Chances to comply

Few people respond well to being stood over. When you want children to do something, especially if you anticipate some resistance, giving some space may increase the rate of compliance. You can do this in several ways:

▶ Say you will come back later to see how they are doing.

▶ Give the magic count of three. It is not clear why this works but it often does! Keep it light as much as possible. A group is likely to respond well so addressing this to more than one child is in your interests. You may not even have to say what will happen when you get to three. If you do, however, get to 'two-and-a-half' then it is as well to clarify the consequence: *If you haven't got your things by the time I get to three you will have to sit on the bench instead of going out.*

▶ You could make this fun and/or alter the parameters by saying *by the time I finish singing this song* or *by the time I come back to this group.*

Encourage communication

Children may express their feelings in actions that get them into trouble. Giving them the vocabulary to communicate what they want and encouraging the use of words is a basic tenet of emotional literacy. Modelling scripts and asking children what they might say is helpful:

▶ *I need you to move so I can see the picture* instead of pushing.

▶ *I was dressing that doll, please give her back* instead of screaming and grabbing.

Other children may not respond positively, of course, and teachers may need to intervene but praising the child for handling a situation calmly will reinforce this.

Helping children out of corners

Children sometimes stubbornly back themselves into psychological 'corners' and teachers need to help them out of these. This means giving them a way to save face. These are some ways to do this:

- ► a space of time to calm down;
- ► an offer to do something together;
- ► asking them what would help;
- ► saying that they could get a drink of water first;
- ► say you might have not said things in a way they understand and you will try a different way;
- ► use 'I' statements so that you express requests that are not accusatory:
  - — *I want you to come in now please.*
  - — *I would like you to show Amber that you are sorry her picture got spoilt — how might you do that so she feels better?*

Consequences as a choice

When a child is being particularly difficult and has not responded to any of the ideas above then offering a choice of consequences is a way of establishing and reinforcing consistent expectations and boundaries. Using this strategy as a first response detracts from its usefulness. Consequence choice should be offered after other attempts have been made to encourage cooperation and preferably not in the height of an emotional outburst where the child is too upset to be able to make decisions or gain from the learning.

Consequences involve telling the child that certain behaviours bring good things and hurtful or unhelpful behaviour will have consequences that are unwanted. It is important to state consequences in terms of the *specific behaviour*, not the child. It is most useful for children to be given 'natural' consequences so that they can see the link between their behaviour and the outcomes. Consequences also need to occur at the time something happens. Telling small children they will get rewarded or get into trouble after an event is much less effective.

CASE STUDY

Dean was playing with Scott in the sandpit. He began to have great fun throwing sand. His early years teacher came and spoke with him about the sand being there for building and digging and that throwing sand might get in his or someone else's eye. This would hurt and he was not to do it. The teacher looked round a minute later to find Dean throwing sand again. This time she gave consequences as a choice: 'Dean, if you play properly with the sand you can carry on having fun in the sand pit with Scott. If you throw sand just one more time then you will come out of the pit and will not be able to play there again until I decide you are ready.'

Dean did throw sand again and was promptly moved out of the pit. Before he was allowed back he was reminded of how he must behave and told that this time he would not have any warnings – he would come straight out if he threw sand and stay out for longer. Dean complied.

Negative consequences should be in line with the policy that has been developed in the centre and agreed by all staff. Any sanctions for behaviour need to be carefully graded. A serious consequence for a first or minor offence leaves nothing for the serious or repeated behaviour.

It is sometimes tempting to offer consequences that are simply not manageable, e.g. 'If you run off with the football one more time you will not be allowed to play with it ever again.' This is the worst possible scenario because children learn to take no notice of what adults say. Give meaningful and manageable consequences carefully – and always follow through!

A note about 'time-out'   Using 'time-out' as a consequence is not uncommon as it removes the child from a stressful situation. It might, however, be better to reframe this strategy so that it is not presented as a 'consequence' or punishment but as a choice. *It might be a good idea if you had some quiet time. Go and choose something to do until you feel better and are able to join in again.*

Control

Some practitioners do not feel comfortable unless they have control over what happens in their centre. If adults make all the decisions, however, there is a risk that children will not develop self-efficacy or an internal locus of control. An external locus of control means that attribution for events is placed outside the individual rather than an appropriate acceptance of responsibility. To develop an internal locus of control children need to feel that their input can make a difference. They therefore need to be given some element of control over their own worlds (see Chapter 2).

Children do need to have confidence, however, that adults are 'in charge', capable of looking after them and knowing what to do in a given situation, including not going to pieces when their behaviour is unacceptable. Without this foundation children are likely to become insecure. Adults who do not display self-control are scary for small children.

Conflict management

People want different things and have different priorities and needs. It is inevitable that conflict will occur from time to time. It is not the existence of conflict that matters but how it is managed. Children can learn very early some of the basic strategies for handling situations by having this shown to them by caregivers.

Conflict between child and adult The child wants something and the adult does not want the child to have it! The adult has a choice here. They can:

▶ Dig their heels in and weather the storm – sometimes necessary, but not always. It is useful, however, to acknowledge that the child is upset and offer comfort.
▶ Capitulate to the child's demands – usually a bad idea – especially if it happens after you have already said a definite 'no'.
▶ Ask the child what they might like instead – a problem-solving conversation.
▶ Offer a compromise solution – stating possible answers and a willingness to negotiate.

The last two model conflict-resolution strategies that inform the child's learning.

Conflict between peers Aim for win/win solutions where there is something in it for both sides. If children are willing to work out an answer themselves you could have peer mediation conversations where each child is given an opportunity to speak and say what they would like. While each child is talking the other listens. They are then asked to brainstorm together all possibilities for a resolution and then decide on one that they are prepared to try.

This does not work unless both children are willing to sort it out. If mediation happens regularly in early years settings it becomes more likely that children will understand what it entails and opt for it.

Changing ourselves

Much of the time we want to change a behaviour that we find unacceptable. However, it is worth remembering that we can only change ourselves and our responses to children. What we do and say, however, makes a difference and small consistent changes over time can have powerful effects.

Celebrate success

When a young child has struggled to learn appropriate behaviour and has made even the smallest step in the right direction, acknowledgement will make a difference to whether or not the child sees the effort as worth it. Everyone needs to be pleased and proud. Share successes with families as part of building their confidence as parents.

SUMMARY OF PART II

Initial responses to unwanted behaviour

Check understanding: Does the child know what to do? Give reminders before reprimands.

Chances to comply: Give the child chances to comply with requests.

Encourage communication: Help children to develop the vocabulary to express what they want instead of physical means.

Avoid corners: Give face-saving opportunities.

Consequences as a choice: Outline the positive outcomes for pro-social behaviour, the sanctions given for unwanted behaviour and give the child the choice. Any rewards need to be attainable and all sanctions both manageable and meaningful – and always followed through. Grade both rewards and sanctions, and agree what these will be in the centre's policy documents.

Control: In order to feel secure, children need to know that adults have control of situations but also that they have some control over what happens to them.

Conflict management: Conflict is inevitable. It is how it is managed that is important. Aim for win/win solutions where there is something in it for both.

Change: We can only change ourselves – but small changes can have powerful effects.

Celebrate success: Everyone needs to be pleased and proud.

III: THE 'P' WORDS FOR THE BIGGER PICTURE

Plans and priorities

A child with difficulties will often have several behaviours that are hurtful or unhelpful. Sometimes you don't know where to start! Don't worry about this. It is not possible to do everything at once and things don't get resolved overnight.

Work out what might be most open to change and plan what you might do to ensure a quick success. This will make you feel more effective and also be a message to the child that she is capable. Other useful targets are those behaviours that underpin others. If a youngster goes around the room upsetting children involved in various activities the target behaviour might be to keep him occupied in one place for a certain length of time.

Focus on the positive

This theme is stressed throughout many books on behaviour and is re-stated here. It is much easier and more effective to focus more strongly on developing the behaviour you want than eliminating behaviour you do not.

Minimal attention to unwanted behaviour and commenting frequently on positive behaviour will reinforce expectations.

The positives and pitfalls of praise

Praise needs to be genuine, brief and specific. Too often children hear 'good boy' rather than receive feedback on exactly what is praiseworthy. If children frequently hear bland praise it gives the impression that they do not have to do much to win approval. It devalues getting it. Make praise worthwhile. Tell children exactly what you are pleased about and relate it to their achievements – comments such as: *Well done Abdul and Adrian for taking turns on the bikes this morning* or *Lisa-Marie, you have worked carefully on your picture, I can see you have drawn earrings.* It is valuable to comment positively on the emotional outcomes as well (see Chapter 4): *It looked as if you were really enjoying the game* or *Completing such a picture must make you feel very proud of yourself.* In time this helps children to realize that achievement and cooperation often lead to good feelings.

Second-hand praise can sometimes be even more valuable than direct acknowledgement. This means telling someone else (usually the parent) what the child has done well, either in the child's hearing or where you know it will get back to them.

Proximity praise   Identify children near to the child who is not behaving as required and praise them for their positive behaviours, cooperation or responsiveness to instruction. Often this will spur imitation and provide an opportunity to give positive and specific feedback to this child as well. It also promotes a sense of belonging in the group.

Personal bests

In a competitive environment some children will always be the losers. This does not help their belief in themselves. Others do not respond well to compliments as these do not fit in with expectations. Some children are only ever told how wonderful they are and never challenged to improve.

Personal bests are a great way for children to get positive feedback for themselves and to stimulate motivation. It is commonplace to talk about athletes achieving a 'personal best' rather than win a race. Introduce this idea to the children and then you can ask them to compare how much better they are doing in various ways than they have done in the past. Some children will respond well to this being presented graphically.

A book of drawings kept over the year can show children just how much they have improved. Something similar can be done for behavioural targets.

'I can' books where individuals write things they can do also focuses children on achievements which they may not even be aware of.

Payback

Often adults insist that a child says sorry to someone they have hurt in some way. Although it is understandable that an apology is considered appropriate (see 'politeness' below) saying sorry is too easy and not always meaningful for children. Under pressure they often almost spit out the word – mainly to avoid further hassle. Young children have an acute sense of fairness. Asking a child how they are going to make someone feel better if they have hurt them, or even things up in some way, not only requires some thought and effort, it also stops the retributions that may otherwise follow. Think about a child 'doing sorry' rather than 'saying sorry'.

Politeness

Social conventions have little to do with being good as such but you may want to encourage the use of 'please', 'thank you' and 'sorry' because these oil the wheels of interaction. They are words of acknowledgement, are easily modelled and help children be viewed more positively – especially by adults. Pretending not to hear requests until the magic 'please' can be fun and non-threatening. Routinely saying 'thank you' *with* children keeps this light but consistent. Modelling saying sorry is better than insisting (see 'payback' above).

Persistence

Once you take action behaviour may deteriorate before it gets better. Don't give up too soon or you will not only be back to square one – things will be even worse! This is especially true when you are suddenly providing a consistent response such as saying 'no' to an unreasonable demand. The whining and tantrums are likely to increase because 'upping the anti' has worked before in that adults get worn down and finally give in. It may take quite a time for the child to realize that this time 'no' means no!

Permission

We are often uncomfortable with the expression of emotion in others but sometimes all we want when we are upset is that someone will recognize our distress – not give us a quick answer to a problem. If a child is crying, don't try and discourage them, demand that they 'cheer up' or question them about 'why'. Say that you can see they are sad and they must have a good reason. If they do not want to speak about it say that when they have finished having a good cry they can join the group again when they feel better. There is more on responding to a distressed child in Chapter 7.

Personal and professional integrity

Emotional literacy and professional integrity are congruent (see Chapter 4). Not taking difficult or defiant behaviour personally, knowing what to do in a situation, and calmly carrying this out in accordance with the principles above will promote everyone's well-being, even if it takes a long time for behaviour to change. Both your self-respect and your credibility will increase when you are handling your job in a way that is professional at all times.

Personal support

If you are in an emotionally literate centre you will feel valued and supported. If that is not the case identify those people you can turn to for constructive conversations and emotional support. It is easier to develop good practice when there is collaboration within the whole centre in which you work (see Chapter 9).

SUMMARY OF PART III

Plans and priorities: It is not possible to do everything at once and things don't get resolved overnight. Start small with the most important issue or the one most open to change.

Being positive: Minimal attention to unwanted behaviour and commenting on positive behaviour will reinforce wanted behaviour.

Praise: Genuine, brief and specific. Second-hand praise is also useful.

Personal bests: When children compete against each other someone is always the loser. When children compete against themselves they are always the winner!

Payback: Saying sorry is too easy and not always meaningful – ask children how they are going to make someone feel better if they have hurt them.

Politeness: Although a social convention, small acknowledgements oil the wheels of positive interactions.

Persistence: Once you take action behaviour may get worse before it gets better. Adults need support to keep it going for long enough. Don't give up too soon.

Permission: Permission to express feelings (safely) helps children calm down faster.

Personal integrity: Staying professional under provocation.

Personal support: It can make all the difference.

SUMMARY

The establishment of cooperative and pro-social behaviour in an early years centre is not anything magical. It is working consistently and collaboratively to a set of clear and agreed principles taking into account the individual and developmental needs of the children. Consider how the principles outlined here may translate in your centre and how you might include them in your own policies and practices.

Other important 'C' words such as being calm, caring and comforting are to be found in Chapter 7.

Chapter 4

Once again with feeling

Emotions are central to the consideration of behaviour: both the feelings that children have and how they are expressed and also the feelings that adults have in response. Children in the early years are developing a sophisticated appreciation of emotion as they learn more about themselves and other people. This chapter deals with how we can support this developmental journey with the establishment of an emotionally literate environment. This includes a 'sense of belonging' and an 'affective curriculum'. There is a focus on developing and maintaining supportive relationships at all levels. 'Significant relationships' are the basis for positive emotional development and pro-social behaviour.

The UK Advisory Group on Education for Citizenship (DfEE 1998) talks about 'young children learning from the very beginning socially and morally responsible behaviour both in and beyond the classroom'. In order to do this they need:

- ▶ a sense of self awareness;
- ▶ a positive self-concept;
- ▶ a sense of others;
- ▶ a feeling of 'belonging';
- ▶ conditions which promote empathy;
- ▶ a learning environment which encourages positive self-expression, including the articulation of emotions;
- ▶ skills of self management;
- ▶ relationship skills;
- ▶ conflict resolution strategies.

This chapter addresses the above as a foundation for pro-social behaviour and in the process models the values of democracy.

THE FEELINGS OF YOUNG CHILDREN

Emotions are an integral part of every day in early years settings – the feelings of the children and the feelings of the adults. One of the delightful aspects of working with little ones is their high level of emotional engagement. Their wide-eyed expressions of awe and wonder, their whole body excitement and surprise and their engaged curiosity can be a highly rewarding part of the job. It is also this unreserved emotional expression that can be most wearing! This ranges from when individuals are simply 'upset' and demanding, to when they are hurtful, defiant and destructive. Here we put these events in a broader context in order to help understand them better and respond more effectively.

The chapter brings the affective element of behaviour, in all its aspects, to the fore. In doing so it addresses the following:

- ▶ the various elements of what we mean when we talk about 'emotion';
- ▶ expectations for the emotional development of young children;
- ▶ what an 'emotionally safe' learning environment looks like;
- ▶ relationship building to enhance a sense of 'belonging';
- ▶ how we might help children to understand and regulate their feelings better;
- ▶ how we can help children express their emotions safely;
- ▶ the value of play in regulation, expression and exploration of emotion;
- ▶ understanding our own feelings in response to certain behaviours;
- ▶ what we need to do in 'listening' to feelings;
- ▶ how to promote the positive for everyone in order to enhance emotional resources and resilience.

WHAT DO WE MEAN WHEN WE TALK ABOUT EMOTION?

Emotions are on a continuum; they encompass positive and gentle feelings of interest, contentment, compassion, comfort, affection and happiness as well as the more overwhelming and disturbing emotions such as fear, anxiety, anger, excitement and sadness. The latter receive most attention because it is the expressions of strong feelings that are often at the root of behaviours that are hard to manage.

As overwhelming emotion is integral to the consideration of child behaviour and adult response it is useful to reflect on what we are talking about. There are many books and different views on the subject and it is not possible here to encompass everything in the debate so we have concentrated on what is most useful for early years practitioners in their everyday work. The following brief synopsis includes:

▶ the physical sensations in emotional arousal;
▶ what emotions are for;
▶ understanding the causes of specific emotions;
▶ emotional expression;
▶ emotional regulation;
▶ reading and responding to emotions in others.

Physical sensations

An emotion is a set of physical sensations we experience in response to environmental cues, usually when something changes. These changes are either a distinct event, such as a stranger suddenly appearing; or a developing situation, such as expecting/needing something which doesn't materialize. Although emotions in young infants begin as an automatic response, by the time they are just a few weeks old cognition within a social context is a highly significant factor. Most of us will have observed a very young baby smiling back at someone. Events are therefore attended to and interpreted (Denham 1998). Emotional responses become increasingly based on judgements, beliefs or expectations that are influenced by the interaction of the following:

▶ whether or not basic needs, including emotional nurturance, are being met;
▶ the perception of what is happening or about to happen;
▶ individuality – especially self-concept, self-esteem, sensitivity to arousal and attention skills;
▶ what is understood about the world based on experiences so far;
▶ what our society and culture says is true or important;
▶ the messages we receive from others, including their emotional states;

53

- ▶ the support networks available;
- ▶ influences such as tiredness and stress on levels of resources;
- ▶ the level and complexity of what is happening – the trigger might be something small that happens to be the 'last straw'.

Powerful emotions can affect our ability to 'think straight'. Daniel Goleman (1996) refers to this as 'emotional hijacking'. It is not possible for anyone, let alone a child, to 'see sense' when their emotions are over-whelming. Sometimes we are not even aware of why we feel so strongly about something because the roots are in early pre-verbal experiences. Emotional memory is increasingly acknowledged as an influential factor in emotional response.

What emotions are for

Emotions are universal and serve many purposes. They are necessary for survival and adaptation, for motivation and for communication and rela-tionship with others (Hyson 1994). Many are culturally dependent. Children learn to be proud or ashamed of what they have been praised or criticized for. Boys who are consistently praised for being 'brave' and not crying when they are hurt may be ashamed of breaking down in tears. We know a discourse of 'belonging' to a certain group can be used to generate pride but also has the potential to undermine compassion and a sense of responsibility towards 'outsiders'.

The emotions we experience are filtered through interpretations just as much as the events themselves. Many of the behaviours that stem from difficult emotions are linked to how individuals interpret something as a threat to their 'sense of self'.

Understanding causes of emotions

Pre-schoolers who have sufficient communication skills can tell you what makes them happy, sad, afraid and angry (Denham and Zoller 1991). Young children do not understand that it is possible to experience conflicting emotions at the same time and may have difficulty discrim-inating between them. Sadness and anger are often confused, particularly in loss situations. Whereas some children may cry pitifully when their parent leaves, others throw themselves into a rage.

Young pre-schoolers are better able to make connections between events and their own feelings but their ability to tune into others increases dramatically between three and five years, especially in a nurturing environment which scaffolds their emotional and social learning.

The expression of emotion

When teachers say they find it difficult to deal with a high level of emotion, they are usually referring to what they consider to be an 'unacceptable' expression of feelings. This is often the crux of 'behaviour management'.

The younger the child, the more of their body is used in the expression of emotion. When they are angry or upset not only is their voice loud, so is the expression on their face! They may use their legs, feet, arms, fists and sometimes their whole body in a passion of rage, despair or frustration. A major temper tantrum is a gripping spectacle.

By the time a child has reached four this behaviour is less likely to occur because most four-year-olds have a broader repertoire of expressions at their disposal and increasingly use language to convey feelings. This, of course, is not much use if others are not prepared to listen! A child who is not able to make his feelings heard and acknowledged is therefore more likely to revert to 'louder' forms of expression where people will take notice. When an infant has learnt that, however much they cry and shout for a response, no one takes any notice they may eventually give up. A passive, silent, sad small child may be thought of as 'good' in that they are not demanding but they are just as needy as others, if not more so.

Sometimes we are surprised when someone suddenly 'loses it'. This may be triggered by the 'last straw' that tips over the accumulation of emotionally loaded events. Difficult emotions surface more easily when tiredness or multiple demands undermine resilience and/or basic needs are not being met. The wise adult will take these factors into account to avoid unnecessary distress.

Emotional regulation

This refers to the ability to change what we feel – mostly to reduce high levels of arousal. All of us have ways of doing this, some more successful in the longer term than others. Sometimes, however, we may need to experience the emotion, name and acknowledge it in order to begin to genuinely become more comfortable.

Regulation of emotion is often linked with social factors. Young children will look to their immediate carers to see if they are expressing fear before responding to the sudden appearance of a large dog, for

55

instance. An initial reaction of alarm may be soothed by the calm response of significant adults or increased by being near someone who panics. Adult modelling of emotional regulation is valuable in helping children reduce the level of agitation they may experience. Adults can also assist in regulating emotions by changing the child's focus. If, for instance, they can point out that the dog looks like a favourite fluffy toy, or that its tail is wagging in a friendly way then this may shift the focus from the dog's size, growl or slobbering jaws!

Another way of regulating emotion is to change our physical positions (Laird and Apostoleris 1996). We do not only smile when we feel happy, we feel happier when we smile! 'Standing tall' really does boost confidence.

Helping young children regulate a high level of emotion

- ▶ Be available – even at a distance.
- ▶ Acknowledge the emotion being expressed.
- ▶ Model your own emotional regulation by staying calm.
- ▶ Move smoothly and talk quietly.
- ▶ Show concern for the child – calm does not mean bland.
- ▶ Reassure the child that they will be OK.
- ▶ Show belief in their ability to calm down themselves/cope with the situation.
- ▶ Offer comfort.
- ▶ Gently change the focus of their attention.

 CASE STUDY

Theo was having a bad day. He didn't get to play with the toy garage because it was Andy's turn and then he tripped up in the playground and got his trousers mucky. He looked very grumpy indeed. Colleen acknowledged his feelings and told him that she was sorry he was having a bad time. Colleen told Theo he had the best example of a grumpy face she'd seen – the eyes were screwed up, the mouth was turned down – she carried out the actions as she talked about them. In no time Theo was laughing at her – and feeling better about his day.

This interaction incorporated several strategies in one: acknowledgement, paradoxical suggestion, humour and the promotion of emotional regulation. For children who are deeply distressed, however, this more light-hearted response is less appropriate.

Reading and responding to emotional expression in others

Young children become increasingly aware of emotional gestures, expressions and body language and may take action on the basis of their reading of these. They may approach someone who is smiling but hide behind a trusted adult if they hear a raised voice.

A toddler may respond to another child being upset by crying themselves. By the time they are four years old, however, children will understand that one person's emotional experience may be different from their own. They may be both querying the cause and perhaps intervening. The way they do that will depend largely on what they have experienced themselves. It is the child who has experienced nurturance who will offer a distressed child a cuddle or a favourite toy. Denham (1996) cites ways in which young children attempt to change sadness and anger in parents. Tuning into the feelings of caregivers is the first stage in the development of empathy and this awareness is worth encouraging. Children's self efficacy will increase if they know that their strategies are well received.

Enhancing development

Children whose emotional development is progressing optimally have caregivers who are not only tuned into the child's emotional communication and needs but also promote their emotional knowledge by acceptance, example and mediation. Less advantaged children need structured opportunities in pre-school but all children can benefit from a higher focus on developing emotional and social competencies. Some very able and well-loved children can throw their weight around regardless of others. They, too, need to develop skills that foster greater self-understanding and more positive relationships.

Before we can begin to focus on the details of teaching and learning, however, we need to look closely at what is involved in establishing and maintaining an emotionally safe environment.

AN EMOTIONALLY SAFE LEARNING ENVIRONMENT

Young children who are emotionally vulnerable and/or challenging may have experienced both inconsistency in adult behaviour and environmental instability. They may have moved from one carer to another, in situations where they have not been able to rely on basic nurturing. Some children may no longer have confidence that their needs will be met or that they will be kept safe. What happens at pre-school can either reinforce these expectations or provide an alternative experience.

An emotionally safe environment promotes:

- ▶ acceptance, belonging and connectedness
- ▶ predictability
- ▶ responsiveness
- ▶ physical and psychological safety.

Helping children feel they belong

Just *being* somewhere doesn't necessarily mean feeling you belong there. This takes time and requires both active intervention to show that your presence is valued and also becoming familiar with:

- ▶ who people are
- ▶ where things are
- ▶ what happens when
- ▶ knowing what to do.

When new children arrive in early years centres they need to be shown where things are and who does what. Pairs of older children can be given the responsibility to introduce them to others, to look after them during their first few days and be there to show them what to do for the following week or so. Asking other children to volunteer as 'play partners' may also be valuable. These simple strategies may relieve anxiety for the newcomer: they also provide children with the opportunity to 'help', to demonstrate care and to be responsible. Expectations should be very clear and an adult on hand to guide where necessary.

Early years centres have many routines. Children may pick these up without structured help but some benefit from being taught what is expected and how to carry it out:

▶ gather the children together with those who have most difficulty listening at the front;

▶ explain carefully and simply what you want them to do;

▶ tell them how you expect them to do it;

▶ demonstrate to the children what you have asked them to do;

▶ ask them to repeat instructions back to you;

▶ get the children to practise what it is you want them to learn;

▶ discuss with the children what they have practised, acknowledging success;

▶ remind the children of expectations each time they carry out this routine;

▶ withdraw prompts gradually but continually to comment on achievement;

▶ use the children's knowledge and skills to help a newcomer to the group learn what is expected;

▶ always remind children what they should be doing before reprimanding them for not doing it.

(Roffey and O'Reirdan 2001)

It enhances fun, belonging and learning when adults carry out routines with deliberate mistakes and ask children to indicate when they get it wrong and what they should be doing.

Equally important is a sense of connectedness. This includes:

▶ feeling that you matter;

▶ knowing things are fair;

▶ being safe and comfortable;

▶ feeling special.

A sense of belonging develops when someone is actively welcomed, included and valued. It is easy to like 'good children' and more challenging to feel positive towards those who are not so amenable. But these children are the ones who need acceptance and affection most and for whom the effort will be most worthwhile. There is evidence that, over time, emotionally positive relationships with teachers can, to some extent, compensate for insecure family environments (Pianta 1992). Relationships are critical to the child's sense of belonging and emotional and social development. The development of such 'significant relationships' underpins the success of any intervention or strategy in promoting pro-social behaviour. Pro-active relationship building also provides good models for interactions.

Demonstrating acceptance and liking

Warmth Looking into a child's eyes and giving them a private smile is a powerful message of interest and warmth. It enhances emotional security. Having a child physically close does the same thing. All children and especially those who are insecure may need to return to a trusted adult over and over again to 'touch base' and adults must expect this to happen.

Appropriate affection Physical affection is also necessary for children's emotional well-being but has been brought into question by well-publicized accounts of inappropriate touching. It is damaging if children who need comfort are refused this but adults should ensure that this always occurs in a public place. Open discussions with families about physical affection and its importance in children's emotional well-being may help to both stem fears and encourage parents to provide this for their children. For some children touching is synonymous with hurting and early years teachers need to tune into the child's preferences and expect ambivalence. Sometimes children will cling and at other times they will push you away. Do not take this personally.

'I' statements Small children believe that when you reprimand them for their behaviour you do not like them. It is therefore helpful if teachers emphasize that it is the behaviour that is unacceptable rather than labelling the child. Use 'I' statements that are general and ensure you let the child know what is wanted, not only what is not, e.g. *Tania, screaming is not allowed here. I do not like anyone screaming. I would like to hear your proper voice, please Tania. Now what is it you wanted to say?*

Separating the person from the problem This is the foundation of narrative approaches. The way you speak to children shows faith and trust in them and refers to how the difficulty they are experiencing is getting in the way of who they really are or what they want: *You seem to be having some trouble with those unkind words again Fanouk. They keep escaping from your mouth and getting you into trouble. What can you do to keep them under control?* Louise Porter (2003) talks to children about their bodies growing up but sometimes their insides haven't caught up yet. Their feelings boss them around and get them into trouble or upset.

Sharing experiences It will help if you go out of your way to make special connection with children you find troubling. Taking the time to talk to them and listen to what they have to say can work towards establishing a 'significant relationship'. Find out about things in their lives that are important to them. See if there is anything you have in common – a similar pet, a TV programme. Children are more likely to imitate social behaviours when they can see some similarity between themselves and the model. It is possible to generate similarities even if there are no obvious ones, e.g. *I liked playing on the climbing frame when I was three, too.*

Keep calm and use a quiet voice when issuing a reprimand. Children pay attention to the volume, tone and pitch of the voice not only the words that are spoken. Shouting at children reinforces their belief that you do not like them. This gives them less motivation to take notice of you and may instil fear.

Other ways to promote a sense of belonging

Develop a sense of fairness   The few rules you establish can be reinforced by reference to fairness: *You can't hit someone in this centre and other people can't hit you.* Put systems in place for the fair distribution of privileges, treats and responsibilities. Lists on the wall is one way, another is names (photos) in a jar that get taken out when that person has had their turn. This not only makes for visible fairness but also is random, showing there are no 'favourites'.

Give each child personal recognition and acknowledgement
Comment regularly on strengths and developing skills: *You can do this now, you have learnt this since last week – well done.*

 CASE STUDY

Henry found it very difficult indeed to sit through the fifteen minutes it took to have a drink, a piece of apple and a short story without poking the children around him. The kindergarten teacher was fed up with telling him to keep his hands to himself so she took a different tack. She told him how long he had managed to behave well, 'Henry, today was a personal best for you, you didn't bother anyone for nearly the whole story.' It wasn't long before Henry saw himself as someone who could sit 'properly' and soon managed the whole activity to applause from the group.

Celebrate differences   You probably have children in your centre with families from around the world. This can be acknowledged in many ways:

▶ place a world map with postcards/photographs pinned on the countries represented in your centre;

▶ have days where children bring in things from home which help tell stories about their community;

▶ ask parents to tell you about games and songs from their childhood that you can in turn teach the children.

Children may have heard racist comments at home. This clearly needs addressing but simply reprimanding children for repeating these is not as helpful as sensitive questioning that encourages reflection. This could include asking children if they felt upset by getting into trouble for something their brother or sister did. Early years educators also need to actively seek opportunities to model tolerance and respect for diversity. Help children understand that familiar things are comfortable but when something is different people may feel anxious or fearful because it is strange to them. Show children that getting to know more about something or someone often takes away the fear. Make a point of mixing up groups for activities so that children play with a wide range of peers.

Show that each child's presence (and absence) matters   Greet children who have been away and let them know they were missed. If a child has been unable to attend a special event for some reason find a way to help them feel included: perhaps getting something relevant from the outing, asking a child to give them a picture or token to make up – even a small wrapped chocolate makes the point. However much you might be tempted avoid saying anything like 'it was nice and quiet without you'! It might be a throwaway light-hearted remark but can deeply undermine a child's sense of safety and belonging.

Ensure each child has their own place and space   This is usually routine for early years centres but it may be valuable to emphasize its importance – perhaps with the use of photographs to identify each child's 'special place'. This is a great way of making children feel they are important. Provide a 'treasure box' where children can safely keep anything they bring from home. It helps confirm that this environment is dependable.

Ensure social inclusion   Some children may be excluded by others in play scenarios because they have not developed sufficient cooperative play skills. Early years practitioners will need to scaffold their inclusion by making suggestions and commentary to facilitate a game, perhaps joining in themselves for a while and promoting an inclusive ethos in which everyone gets a go. Older pre-school children can be introduced to the idea of a 'play stop'. This is a particular place, usually in the playground, where children stand if they have not got anyone to play with. It is up to others to 'pick up' such children as they go past so that they can join in with the game.

Some early years centres have introduced a 'You can't say you can't play' rule that addresses the behaviour of the group rather than the behaviour of the isolated child. Vivian Paley (1992) asserts that whereas children may choose their friends at home, school is for everybody and social exclusion not appropriate. She reports some initial complaints from the children but finds that there are positive longer-term outcomes. The process of inclusion is relevant. Children become more accepting in their attitudes towards others when group activities promote awareness, challenge stereotypes, and encourage interaction.

Excluding small children from fun events because their behaviour may be problematic should be the very last resort. How flexible can you be so they can be included?

Providing opportunities for children to help each other   It is important that the less able children also have this opportunity rather than always being the recipient. 'Helping' becomes an important aspect of friendship in middle childhood – giving pre-schoolers opportunities to practise stands them in good stead.

Developing a sense of group pride   The word 'we' needs to promote togetherness not the exclusion of others. A group collage that includes pictures of all the children and entitled: 'We are the Green Class' or 'We all belong to the Tigers Group' is a visible sign of group identity. 'This class can . . .' or 'likes to . . .' with a collage of activities develops this. Individual pictures could promote inclusion together with the positive, e.g. 'Francine is in our class. She joins in with the singing.' 'Denny belongs in our group. He helps Sarah tidy up.' Children can perhaps choose what is written about themselves.

Sharing the good times If the whole group can regularly laugh together this will not only generate positive emotions and provide stress relief but also foster connectedness. Early years teachers have access to a wealth of funny poems and group games that are enjoyable to share together. Another idea is to refer back to shared times: 'Remember when . . .' emphasizes a history of belonging together.

The importance of predictability

Vulnerable children often have difficulty with the unexpected. For some, even transitions from one activity to another can present a threat. Predictability means that children will know what is happening, be able to anticipate responses and can depend on people doing what they say they will do.

Well-defined and clearly communicated routines are useful. If these are depicted visually this is even better (see Chapter 5). When children know what is happening they can begin to explore from this secure base. It is unnecessary to stick rigidly to a routine but important to be aware of what deviations may mean for some children. Giving fore-warning when changes might be expected may deflect any potential upset. Small children do need challenges and new experiences but introducing these carefully with an element of familiarity can inhibit feelings of insecurity.

Children need to rely on what adults say. Some individuals will have learnt to take minimal notice of what they hear, both positive and nega-tive, because they can never rely on it. Early years professionals have to be scrupulous in coming up with the goods and take great care about what they say in the first place!

Minimizing a sense of failure

Some children become very fearful of making mistakes if they have been punished or belittled for getting things wrong – or they might just be perfectionists; many children are. Accepting mistakes as part of learning is fundamental to an emotionally safe environment. Children can be asked: *How might you do that differently next time?* or *Is there anything else you could have done?*

When early years practitioners model acceptance of failure for them-selves this can have a powerful impact. This includes:

- saying on occasions that you could have done something better;
- making mistakes sometimes and letting children 'help' get it right;
- apologizing sometimes;
- problem-solving out loud to show there are alternatives to many things and it is often not a question of 'right or wrong' but working out what is a better option;
- commenting on what you have learnt from something that didn't go right.

Addressing bullying

An emotionally safe environment will pro-actively address the issue of bullying. This includes name-calling, exclusion, intimidation and/or physical attack regularly perpetrated by one person or group onto an individual. It is common for children who bully to target those who are obviously different from others or in some way less able to defend themselves. It is not helpful for children to be labelled either as a bully or as a victim, but bullying behaviour requires a high profile for several reasons:

- children who are bullied become fearful and miserable or learn to bully others;
- it reduces self-esteem and self-efficacy;
- allowing such behaviour to go unchecked reinforces it;
- there are poor long-term outcomes for everyone involved;
- it is an issue of social justice.

An early years centre that is successfully addressing bullying will:

- have discussed what is meant by bullying behaviour;
- acknowledge that bullying behaviour is unacceptable;
- have clear expectations for behaviour;
- actively promote positive behaviour;
- provide opportunities for children to talk about what they might do to make sure that children don't hurt each other and what this means;
- make clear to children and families that physical, verbal and psychological aggression will always be taken seriously;
- have consistent responses from staff when children report bullying behaviour;

- ▶ supervise all areas where bullying might take place;
- ▶ have staff who model emotionally literate interactions including in their responses to bullying behaviour;
- ▶ have a policy in place that is regularly monitored and reviewed.

Teaching children how to sort out bullying themselves in the first instance empowers them and teaches appropriate assertiveness.

 CASE STUDY

One early years centre teaches children three statements. They are expected to use each in turn, before going to an adult. At statement two the situation is considered to be one of bullying and a teacher will intervene if the behaviour does not stop after statement three. It works well.

1 I don't like you doing that.
2 I need you to (e.g. leave me alone).
3 If you don't stop I will get someone to help me.

Another centre teaches the younger children to put up a hand in front of them and just say 'stop'. This simple assertive gesture can be very empowering.

The 'no-blame' approach to bullying is worth trying before bullying behaviour is entrenched. Children are not blamed and details of incidents not discussed. The small group involved (or the perpetrator and a few others) is told that someone is very unhappy at the moment and needs some help to feel better. The conversation can perhaps be supported by drawings that the child has done about feeling sad or lonely. The group is asked what they could do to help. Each individual child says what he or she will do, if necessary with ideas prompted by the teacher. The child who has been bullied is then invited in to hear and comment on the things that each person is offering to help them feel happier. The intervention is checked and monitored daily in the first instance and then less regularly. The children are all given positive feedback for their kindness and helpfulness (Maines and Robinson 1992).

THE DEVELOPMENT OF EMOTIONAL AND SOCIAL COMPETENCE IN YOUNG CHILDREN

An emotionally safe environment supports children in processing emotions rather than being overwhelmed by them. This allows for the optimal development of emotional understanding and skills.

The domains of social and emotional development are interdependent. The development of emotional competencies in the early years is crucial for the ability to develop positive social relationships and the quality of children's relationships is central to their emotional development and well-being. These relationships are complex and multi-dimensional including 'connectedness, shared humour, balance of control, intimacy and shared positive emotions' (Dunn 1993: 113). Children need to both tune into and regulate the emotions experienced in interactions in order to establish and maintain relationships with their peers. It is the emotionally aware and skilled child who makes friends easily in pre-school. This includes being positive, inclusive, empathic and confident (Rubin 1980).

An 'emotional curriculum' includes:

▶ helping children develop awareness of feelings;
▶ learning how to talk about feelings and promoting an 'emotion' vocabulary;
▶ guiding children in ways to regulate their feelings;
▶ promoting positive feelings;
▶ helping children work out difficult feelings;
▶ developing empathy.

The processes to put this in place are:

▶ modelling of good emotional management;
▶ emotional commentary and 'coaching';
▶ talking about emotions;
▶ opportunities for interactions with others;
▶ access to play opportunities, especially 'pretend play';
▶ appropriate responses to children's expressed emotions;
▶ scaffolding of emotional 'problem-solving'.

Over time children come to understand that everyone has emotions, that these are linked to different situations and that there is more than one reason to have certain feelings. They also learn that emotions are communicated by gestures, expressions and words and that there are different ways of showing feelings. Children learn that not everyone is the same and that their peers may be happy or upset by different things and also comforted by different things.

The everyday interactions in the early years environment are where concepts are developed and emotional strategies practised. An 'emotional curriculum' is not the provision of formal targeted activities but an integrated experience that builds children's understanding of themselves and others.

'Emotional modelling' needs to occur throughout the day. Emotions are contagious. If a teacher is enthusiastic the children are more likely to be, if she is angry and irritable they will be more upset. Adults who demonstrate concern provide models for caring behaviour. What early years practitioners do and say, the ways they respond to their own feelings and those of others and the conversations they have are the most influential component of an emotional curriculum.

Although clear direction is often important, simply telling children what to do does not establish the inner knowledge nor the motivation to develop emotional skills. It is 'wondering' rather than interrogative questioning and 'reflective commentary' that help connect thinking, feeling and action. The type of conversations that early years professionals have with children are central. These conversations need to provide opportunities for children to:

▶ reflect
▶ consider alternatives
▶ problem-solve
▶ enhance their imaginative thinking
▶ take responsibility.

Early years professionals who ask searching but age-appropriate questions will find that even very small children can make thoughtful decisions given the chance.

The following presents some of the opportunities in a pre-school setting for focusing on how children feel and developing their social and emotional understanding and competence.

Adult labelling of emotions, modelling of regulation and expression and request for help   Evidence suggests that this is the most effective way of helping children develop empathy (Denham 1998) and other social/emotional competencies. The words said need to be accompanied by the appropriate facial expressions and gestures. Children with limited vocabulary may rely on this form of communication and it reinforces language for able children.

RAISING AWARENESS OF FEELINGS FOR CHILDREN

'You enjoyed that funny little poem didn't you? Would it make you happy if I read it again?'

'Brendan is angry that his painting is spoilt. Would you be angry if it was your painting?'

'Chi, was it exciting to go to the circus?'

'Mel is hanging her head. She is sad that she didn't win the race.'

'This is a picture of Isa. She used to live in another country but because there was a lot of fighting, it wasn't safe there. She had to leave with her mum and dad. What do you think she might be feeling?'

COMMENTARY ON THE EMOTIONAL COMPONENT OF EXPERIENCES

'Please be careful when you run around, it hurt when you ran into me.'

'My cat is sick today and I am sad that she is not feeling well.'

'I saw someone fall off his bike today and I was relieved when he stood up again and was all right.'

'Sebastian, you took turns in that game this morning very nicely. I am so happy you were able to do that. Do you feel pleased with yourself too?'

COMMENTARY ON FINDING WAYS TO FEEL BETTER

'I was so upset that my team lost the match that I went out for a long walk – and I kicked all the leaves on the ground and didn't feel so bad after that.'

'I missed my bus last night and was cold and tired and miserable when I got home – so I made myself a cup of tea and had a hot bath and felt much better.'

'I was cross that this picture kept falling off the wall – but when I tacked it up with staples rather than with tape it was OK. I was really pleased I found something that worked.'

There was a big spider in my bath which made me scared because I don't like spiders. But I was quite brave and went and got a glass, put it over the spider like this, slid a piece of cardboard under it like this and then took it outside and let it go. I felt proud of myself and I won't be scared next time because I know what to do.'

REQUEST FOR HELP

'I am worn out picking up all this paper. Who could help me?'

'I am sorry but you can't play with that – it's too dangerous. I am scared you will hurt yourself. I need you to put it down and find something else. Now, what would be a safer thing to play with?'

'I have a bit of a headache today, so I need you to practice your little voices if you can. Who can remember to do that?'

Empathy begins when children show concern towards and meet the needs of those who have a significant relationship with them. It is valid for children to be asked to show some consideration for parents and caregivers within a framework of fairness. This will encourage the child to realise that while their needs are important, so are the needs of others. Without this simple intervention children may learn that only they matter. This is not in the interest of their future good relationships.

Puppets

Puppets can be used to express emotions that are more difficult to do in person. The narratives in puppetry are controlled by the adult but the indirect nature of this interaction can open up imaginative pathways for children. Puppets should not be used by adults to show fighting and aggression but used to help with problem-solving.

Puppet 1:	I have hurt myself in a fight and it is sore. I don't want to feel hurt.
Puppet 2:	I was in the fight and I got hurt too. I don't want to get hurt.
Puppet 1:	I thought it was your fault, but then I thought it was my fault too. We both got into the fight.
Puppet 2:	Do the children get into fights? I wonder what they fight about?

Children contribute:

Puppet 1:	Do you get hurt too? That's not nice for you.
Puppet 2:	Let's pretend we did something else and we didn't get hurt.
Puppet 1:	What do you think children? What shall we pretend?

And so on – the possibilities are endless.

CONSIDERATION CAN BE ELICITED BY THE ADULT (a) MAKING THEIR OWN NEEDS CLEAR AND (b) OFFERING AN INCENTIVE

'I need two children to wash out all the paint brushes for me – who can do this carefully and be my "paint pot stars" for today?'

'I want to watch the last of this programme. Would you like to cuddle up here while I do that?' You may want to be even more generous to ensure a positive outcome: 'Then perhaps we will go to the playground for half an hour.'

SCAFFOLDING PROBLEM-SOLVING

'Now you can't find your coat. I can see you are upset. What do you think we might do? Let's think where you saw it last. If it isn't there perhaps someone has tidied it away. Where would they put something away? Could you go and look in all those places. Is it there? Well done. Next time you will know what to do before you get upset.'

'You don't like it when Angel pushes into your game. It makes you angry. What could you do instead of punching her? What could you say? Perhaps just saying "I am playing this game, you have to ask to join in."'

Pictures and books

Young children are, of course, very visual. There are now many useful books targeted for young children that focus either on feelings or on emotionally challenging situations. There are also cards such as the Bear Cards, which depict feelings and relationships. All of these can be used as prompts for conversations and reflective thinking. A resource list is given at the end of this chapter.

Young children also have opportunities to express emotional and emotionally laden situations in drawings and paintings. Simple commentary may provide children with the opportunity to explore and experiment with their feelings and perhaps problem-solve in an indirect way: *This little girl is sitting by herself. Is she OK? What do you think she would like to happen next?*

Another excellent way of encouraging emotional awareness and providing a context for talking about feelings is to play different kinds of music while children use creative materials. Ask them to draw a picture that makes them feel like the music.

Cooperative interactions

The early years environment provides a powerful incentive to regulate and safely express emotions because many children will avoid others whose outbursts they find alarming. In order to engage in cooperative play children need to learn to modify displays of anger, distress and uncontrolled excitement. Early years professionals may help them to do this by:

- ▶ Pointing out their desire to play with others and what they need to do to facilitate this: *You want to play with George but George doesn't like it when you jump on him like that.*
- ▶ Ask what they would want if they were the other children: *What could you do so George will want to play with you?*
- ▶ Explore what they might do to express feelings safely: *If you feel like jumping up and down where's a good place to do it?*

Pretend play

Children in early childhood often use dramatic and symbolic play scenarios to work out emotions and explore ways of managing them. Play scenarios give children the chance to control their environment. They can experiment and imagine and practise many ways of dealing with situations and experiencing emotions. All they need is a few symbolic play props and the opportunity to interact with others. Although early years professionals can scaffold situations, it is important to be child-led here. Giving children too much input limits their own imaginative development.

Acting out violence

Sometimes pretend play includes scenarios that are difficult for teachers to tolerate. Rather than directly stopping these, it may be better to provide commentary and where possible develop a non-judgemental, problem-solving conversation: *The daddy is smacking the baby. Is the baby upset? The baby is crying. Will smacking stop the baby crying? What could we do instead to stop the baby crying? What would help you to stop crying? A cuddle? Let's try that.*

If children are involving others in violent play and they are getting hurt this is unacceptable and undermines the safety of the centre. The phrase: *You are not allowed to hurt anyone here, no one is allowed to hurt you* is appropriate.

Guns and superheroes

Children, especially boys, often want to be 'superman' or a 'special-forces fighter'. What do you do if you don't approve of guns, even toy ones? There are different views about this. Penny Holland (2003) has explored this dilemma and discovered that 'zero tolerance' of such fantasy play was not necessarily the best way to go. Children are presented with violent media images in the news and may need opportunities to respond to these and to experiment with feeling powerful in the face of potential fear. Accepting elements of such games can provide opportunities for early years professionals to mediate this fantasy play without simply making hard and fast moral judgements. Practitioners may also want to encourage girls to participate in games where they have the chance to role-play powerful characters.

Play that is simply repetitive of violent themes does not offer an opportunity for reflection and is best limited or re-directed. It is also useful to restrict superhero games to certain places or within certain times so that they do not become dominant in the centre. Get children to practise some game moves carefully, pretending they are 'stunt' actors (Gronlund 1992). This reinforces that this is fantasy and that people are not to get hurt for real. There are simple picture books (e.g. Popov 1995) which enable educators to bring another measure of reflection into war games.

Role-play

Most children love doing this. There are several different kinds. One is an extension of pretend play when children can try out being different people. Providing 'dressing up' clothes and accessories may be all they need to act out their own narratives.

Teachers can help structure role-play for children by getting them to act out stories either from books or ones that they develop with the children. This provides the choice of characters that children might otherwise not consider developing.

Another, more structured, activity is to give children opportunities to carry out activities and/or express their emotions 'the silly way' and then the 'right way'. Children find it very funny to see the adults act like 'naughty' children. This, together with role-playing the 'correct' way, reinforces what is acceptable, making it an excellent learning tool.

'Use your words'

This simple phrase bears frequent repetition in the early years setting. Children need to learn to express their emotions and what they want with words, not with fists, grabbing and shoving. Questions to reinforce this practice can include: *what do you need?*; *what did you tell him?*; *how did he know?*

Other imaginative scenarios

Young children's imagination is often an untapped source of possibilities, including for regulating emotion. An adult can respond to a request from a child for something with a mime and many children will join in with the game.

 CASE STUDY

Saffron had waited long enough for the little car in the playground. She came up for the third time and said 'I want a go, when is it my turn?' Dom, the early years teacher, knew that there were two others in line before Saffron. He said 'Hey, here's another one while you wait' and mimed getting into a car and holding the steering wheel and squealing round corners. When he said 'Do you want to get in and drive?' Saffron was quite willing and even involved another child as a passenger in the pretend car.

THE POWER OF THE POSITIVE

There is increasing evidence that a focus on the positive supports emotional regulation and enhances resilience. The ability to 'bounce back' from or cope with stressful situations is linked with being able to identify what is positive (Frederickson *et al.* 2000). This can be a learning outcome, an opportunity or a new way of seeing something. Whereas negative emotions limit creativity, positive emotions broaden the exploration of coping strategies and build personal resources (Frederickson and Tugade 2004). Helping young children to begin to develop the ability to focus on the positive is therefore worthwhile.

Positive emotions can also be elicited by using humour, relaxation techniques and optimistic thinking.

PROMOTING THE POSITIVE

Asking children to focus on their feelings when things are going well:

You feel good inside when you are stroking the rabbit, Josh, is that right?

Helping children to remember good feelings:

Remember when we went to the zoo. Everyone was so excited.

Helping children to focus on the good feelings linked with positive behaviours:

We were all excited but we also felt safe because we held hands to stay together.

You were really happy playing that game together once you had worked out the rules.

Asking children, with appropriate prompts, what they have learnt from a negative experience:

You were scared but the car missed you and you did not get run over. What did you learn here to keep you safe next time?

CIRCLE TIME

The children sit in a circle with the early years teacher acting as facilitator. The younger the children, the shorter and more frequent the sessions need to be. Circle time is a democratic and inclusive forum to raise self-esteem, promote belonging and develop emotional and social understanding and skills. It lasts 15–20 minutes, depending on the children's ability to participate. Children may need time to get used to circle time but persistence pays off. Those children who initially pass will eventually join in. Circle time has three rules:

▶ listen if someone else is speaking (use a soft toy or wand to indicate whose turn it is – some children feel easier speaking through a puppet);

▶ only saying good things about people (no put-downs);

▶ you can pass if you don't want to join in when it is your turn.

A circle time session on the theme of 'feeling happy' might look like this in the box:

Introductory activity

Verbal: e.g. say your name/your friend's name/the name of brothers or sisters.

Non-verbal: e.g. pass a smile around the circle – or a hand squeeze.

Sentence completion activity

Each child completes the sentence in turn e.g. 'I am happy when . . .'

Mix-up game

The idea is that children communicate with all the children in their group not just the same few. There are hundreds of ways of doing this, e.g. all those who like chocolate ice-cream change places. Give children animal names and ask the animals to change places.

Share pair

With the person next to you, find out e.g. two things you both like to play with. Each child feeds back one thing to the circle.

Game

A physical, fun activity using positive energy, e.g. teacher gives each child a part in a story – this can include characters and inanimate objects. The teacher tells the story and every time she mentions a character or object that person stands up, turns round and sits down. When she says: . . . *and everyone was very happy* all the children change places.

A calming activity

A short quiet story, relaxation activity, quiet music with 'mind pictures' or a quiet game.

Collins and McGaha (2002) suggest that even with toddlers circle time can be beneficial. This study stresses that the process of getting it going in the early years requires flexibility and needs to be child led. Children who are too absorbed in other activities should be left to continue with them. They are likely to choose to join in once they see that others are having a good time. One adult needs to stay with the circle while another supports children in their efforts to make the transition or in their other choices. Smooth continuous activity in the circle is maintained if children who are unwilling or unable to participate are given the option to be self-directed. Once circle time becomes a power struggle with continual stoppages or criticisms it loses purpose and value.

Children are likely to want to touch materials that are brought into circle time – it will help their participation if they are encouraged to do so – especially if there are several items. This can also help when children are waiting for their turn.

RESOURCES FOR AN EMOTIONAL LITERACY CURRICULUM IN THE EARLY YEARS

I Can Monsters
Bear Cards
Stones Too Have Feelings

All the above are picture cards published by St Lukes Innovative Resources. They also have a selection of other useful materials: www.innovativeresources.org.

The National Association for the Education of Young Children has books and multi-media training kits such as *What do you do with the mad that you feel*: www.naeyc.org.

Nikolai Popov is the artist for the picture book *Why?* published in the US by North-South Books. This powerfully illustrates how conflict escalates and why this is in no one's interest. This is also available from Peoplemaking in Australia 03 9813 2533.

Margaret Collins's book *Circle Time for the Very Young* published by Lucky Duck has lots of ideas for circle time activities: www.lucky-duck.co.uk.

There has not been sufficient space here to discuss gender issues in the development of emotional literacy. Don Kindlon and Michael Thompson's book *Raising Cain: Protecting the Emotional Life of Boys* published by Penguin is well worth reading, especially the first two chapters.

SUMMARY

Young children are on a steep learning curve, discovering many things about themselves and about each other. Supporting and enhancing their social and emotional understanding and competencies within an emotionally safe environment will impact on their behaviour and their ability to establish good relationships with others. This is the beginning of the upward spiral to social inclusion.

Chapter 5

Learning, language and behaviour

Many behaviours that early educators find challenging are where children are either operating at a level expected of a much younger child or they have a specific difficulty, often with language development and communication skills. There is evidence that behaviour difficulties and learning problems have a 40–50 per cent overlap (Hinshaw 1992). There are also indications that language difficulties are often overlooked with the focus for intervention on behaviour only (Cross 2004). About 80 per cent of those with communication difficulties are male. This chapter outlines what these difficulties might be, how to recognize them and where to go next. In light of the fact that so many young children have intermittent conductive hearing loss, many of the strategies given here are useful generally for early years centres.

Emotional development, language development and social development are interdependent:

▶ Children can only be cooperative if they understand what is being asked of them.
▶ Children with learning/language difficulties may be confused, jump to conclusions and find it hard to predict what is expected.
▶ Children may try to make sense of what is going on and not always get this right.
▶ Skills that other children learn 'automatically' need to be specifically taught.
▶ Children who are unable to communicate effectively become frustrated and find other ways, often physical, to make their needs known.

▶ Children who cannot conceptualize or express emotions in words have fewer strategies for emotional regulation.

▶ Children need the foundations for communicative interaction if they are to function well in a group – making friends is not easy.

▶ Having the words to structure thinking underpins the ability to problem-solve.

▶ In order to develop positive social interactions and function in groups, children need to understand that they are different from others and that others have separate needs, thoughts and emotions. Although this is applicable to all young children, those with learning needs and those on the autistic spectrum have particular difficulty.

Communication becomes second nature to children whose skills are developing well. It takes so much more effort for those who have a language and/or learning difficulty. Everything is harder for them. It can be exhausting trying to pick up clues from everywhere to work out what is going on, let alone getting others to understand you. It is not surprising that some children 'tune out' and others 'act out'.

GENERAL LEARNING NEEDS

Some children develop at a more leisurely pace than others. With serious learning difficulties the child is likely to remain developmentally delayed and will not 'catch up' with their peers. Sometimes such difficulties are obvious, such as children with Down syndrome. More often there is a slow process of comparison, awareness, worry and realization. Early years staff are often the ones to raise the concern with parents and this is often because the child's behaviour is not the same as the others in the group. Any assessment and discussion needs to be handled with great sensitivity and empathy. You are in effect raising with parents the prospect that the child they thought they had is no longer there. They may be very upset for themselves and their child and may also be angry with you. It is important not to take this personally or to try to 'make' the parent realize their child's needs (see Chapter 8 for ways of discussing this with care).

Indications that a four-year-old may have long-term learning needs include:

▶ major milestones achieved significantly later than other children;

- ▶ plays alone or in parallel with others rather than in cooperative games;
- ▶ restricted or repetitive play skills rather than engaging in spontaneous and diverse activities;
- ▶ little evidence of imaginary or complex play scenarios;
- ▶ has poor basic social skills;
- ▶ needs more assistance than others in self-help skills;
- ▶ needs to have more practice than others to learn new things;
- ▶ is more 'physical' and less verbal than others of the same age;
- ▶ has fragmented attention skills, finds it difficult to focus;
- ▶ seeks affection indiscriminately;
- ▶ may be very passive and not eager to engage with the environment.

Unsurprisingly, some of the above lead to behaviours that are not easy to manage in an early years setting. Such children are often self-directed, not responsive to adult instruction and may strongly resist direction. It is essential that they are not blamed but supported in achieving their potential.

Taking action

What is appropriate   Having developmentally inappropriate expectations for a child is frustrating to adults and sows the seeds of failure for the child. It is important to work out where the child is at so that you can support their learning and development at the right level. The brief early years assessment here gives you some simple guidance in this. More detailed planning for special education needs can be found in *Special Needs in the Early Years* (Roffey 2001).

What is the next step   Once you have worked out what the child can do without help, you need to work out what the emerging skills are – these are things the child can do with help or under certain circumstances, also known as the zone of proximal development (Vygotsky 1978).

Where do you focus   What is most useful to the child in the centre? For behavioural issues try the behaviour that is most open to change first. This gives the child success and you some satisfaction! You might

BRIEF EARLY YEARS ASSESSMENT GUIDE

Along with discussions with parents, observation provides good information. What is the child able to do with and without help/in which circumstances? What are emerging skills? What is already helping the child move on? What might be good areas to focus on?

Play skills

► At what level of complexity are play scenarios?

► What evidence is there of imaginative and symbolic play?

► How varied is the child's choice of play materials/activities?

► To what extent does the child play in parallel, interactively or collaboratively?

► What fine and gross motor skills are evident in play?

Social interactions

► In which ways/in which activities does the child interact with others?

► Do they stand and watch or want to get involved? How do they try and join in?

► In which ways does the child follow others or take initiatives?

► In which circumstances can the child share/take turns/follow rules of a game?

► Is the child motivated to participate in group activities? What helps with this?

Communication

► What supports the child's listening skills?

► In which ways do they communicate needs/interest/feelings?

► What do you know about their level of understanding of language?

► If bilingual, what are their skills in their own language?

► What motivates their communication?

Response to direction

▶ How many pieces of information can the child manage at one time?

▶ What helps them follow directions? Can they copy a model?

▶ To what extent is the child able to follow directions given to a group?

▶ When is their concentration at its best and what supports this?

▶ Are they able to complete a task? What helps?

Independence

▶ What does the child want to do for himself?

▶ What can they currently manage in dressing/toileting/eating/ other skills?

▶ How do they manage frustration?

▶ Is there evidence of problem-solving?

Likes/dislikes

▶ What activities are most chosen? What does this indicate?

▶ What does the child appear to find most challenging?

▶ What does the child avoid? Are there clear reasons for this?

Emotional competencies

▶ What helps in calming them down when they are excited?

▶ What helps in calming them down when they are upset?

▶ How does the child express feelings? Do they use words and in which circumstances?

▶ In which ways do they talk about the feelings of others?

▶ When is the child able to identify positive feelings?

also want to address issues that underpin some of the behavioural difficulties – such as taking turns.

How do you do it   You will know that the best way of helping children develop new skills is to show them how and encourage them. If you wanted to help a child take turns in a game, for instance, you might do that with them first before introducing another child as a threesome and then opting out to see how they get on. For a child who is self-directed it is best to join in with what interests them and extend their skills from there rather than try and impose your own agenda. Children who have learning difficulties need to have targets in smaller, more manageable steps than others.

What can you ignore   Children who are operating at a different developmental level than others require some flexibility in your approach – you would not expect the same from a two-year-old as you would a three-and-a-half-year-old. There will be things you must address but there will be things it is more sensible to let go. Decide with colleagues in order to have a consistent approach.

Helping children communicate   This is a crucial issue addressed in the next section.

LANGUAGE NEEDS

Language difficulties come in several guises:

▶   Some children have delayed language skills both in their understanding of the spoken word and also in their ability to express themselves. This can either be connected with a general learning difficulty or because they have experienced little interactive communication at home. These children have a small functional vocabulary and may not understand many of the words used in an early years centre.

▶   If language difficulties are part of a pattern of other concerns such as strong fear of change and ritualistic behaviours children may be on the autistic spectrum. Behaviour can be difficult to understand and hard to manage.

▶   Other children have a specific language difficulty. Different parts of the brain deal with the different language processes and specific language difficulty is an impairment in just one area. Sometimes, because children appear to express themselves quite well, assumptions are made about their comprehension. They will nod and say 'yes' without understanding and then get in trouble for 'misbehaving'.

▶ Social communication difficulties are where children can talk but their associated interactive skills are poor. They do not tune into context, perhaps make poor eye contact, do not understand conversational patterns or responses and do not infer pragmatic social skills, such as how to join in a game.

▶ Language may be impaired because of hearing loss. Children often can hear sounds but not make out what the words mean because they only hear part of them. Usually it is high frequency sounds that get lost – this means hearing the vowels in words but not many of the consonants. Sometimes children are said to 'hear me when she wants to' when in fact they can only make out words if they are able to lip-read. Make sure you are facing the child and not in silhouette.

▶ Articulation difficulties are where children can speak but not make themselves understood because the sounds don't come out right. When adults walk away because they cannot make out what is being said the child may believe that the person doesn't like them. Try to identify and respond to at least one word.

▶ Selective mutism. Children can understand and use language but lack the confidence to communicate in words or have had experiences that inhibit language.

Language is only part of the child – how confident and sociable they are will also impact on their behaviour. Some children want desperately to communicate and may get very frustrated by not being able to do this easily. Others are prepared to take a back seat and only communicate when others attempt to interact. Some are reluctant to engage at all. Individual strengths and needs must be part of the package of intervention if this is to be effective.

The way adults interact with children is a crucial component of how well they are able to communicate effectively. This includes following the child's lead, being patient and structuring alternatives where possible and appropriate. The child's self-esteem is very vulnerable. Unless they have the good fortune to have adults who intervene effectively they are potentially faced with daily failure. Children may become very good at picking up environmental clues and can therefore give the impression that they understand more language than they do. Early years staff need to be aware of this.

Taking action

Language is symbolic – it represents the 'real' world. We develop language as we connect sounds we hear with what they stand for. It is not a simple process. We have to hear the word that is said, recognize it, recognize what it means, hold it with other words and then take it to another part of the brain to say it.

Children who have limited language skills need to have the world explained to them in ways that make sense. If you support the comprehension you support the behaviour. This means providing concrete, graphic or physical connections. Children need to have either the real thing that the words apply to, visual representations or other ways of understanding. They also need to have access to materials to enable them to communicate what they need to say. If you have ever been in a country where you don't speak the language you will appreciate how much you rely on other clues to let you know what's going on – and how scary it is when they are not there. Anyone who has been faced with a red-faced ticket collector shouting at you in a language you don't understand and clearly expecting you to respond in a certain way will have some idea what these children might be feeling every day. If you felt like yelling back at him or stomping off without doing the 'right' thing you will have sympathy with the child who develops challenging behaviour.

The answer lies in:

▶ helping children to communicate in different ways, providing them with alternatives/support for spoken language;
▶ observing closely how each individual is trying to communicate in order to support their emerging skills;
▶ giving contextual and visual support to communicate what is required;
▶ not overloading children with information;
▶ being patient with their efforts, acknowledging the demands it makes on them.

Restricted commentary on action   Children learn language by being immersed in it and needing it to interact with others. An early years teacher who is playing with a small child will be using a running commentary, e.g. *The farmer is standing by the sheep. He has got a sheep dog too. The sheep dog is running round and round the sheep. Where is the farmer's tractor? The farmer goes in the big red tractor. He is driving all round the field. Perhaps the dog should follow the farmer – here we go.* A child who has a language difficulty needs fewer words, more emphasis, more repetition and larger-than-life actions: *Here's the farmer, here's the sheep, here's the farmer's dog. Here's the tractor. Into the tractor goes the farmer. Round the field goes the farmer in the tractor. Round the sheep. Here comes the dog.*

Gestures and expressions   If you watch a signer you will notice that not only do they use their hands to speak but their entire bodies are engaged in the process. All of this provides additional cues to language. Pointing is a great gesture! If, however, a child is on the autistic spectrum they may be sensitive to sensory overload and not respond well to additional stimuli. The child is likely to indicate when something is too much for them – perhaps by putting their hands over their ears or eyes.

Make statements rather than asking questions   The posing of a question might be challenging for a child with language difficulties – it is better to make statements, e.g. rather than ask *Liam, what are you doing?* say *Liam, you are under the table.*

Routines and sequences   It is helpful for all children to be clear about routines. For children with a learning or language difficulty picture/photo sequences assist their understanding of what is to happen. With a picture sequence of the day, the early years worker can point to the picture as she says *it is time to go outside now.* Giving forewarning in pictures about changes in routine also helps prepare children and reduces anxiety.

Social stories   Often used for children on the autistic spectrum and with Asperger syndrome, social stories can be used for any child who needs visual representations of events. There are ready-made social stories on the market (e.g. Gray 2002) but even better are those that have been developed to meet individual needs.

CASE STUDY

Brendan loved the box of play people in the early years centre. He was allowed to play with it at the end of the morning but then had great difficulty putting it away. Every day he threw a major tantrum. Jen, his key worker, drew a social story with Brendan that helped him understand what was going to happen every day:

Picture 1: Brendan and his dad coming into the centre.

Picture 2: Brendan playing outside with other children.

Picture 3: Brendan having a drink and fruit.

Picture 4: Jen taking the play people down from the shelf.

Picture 5: Brendan playing with the play people.

Picture 6: Brendan looking sad because it is time to clear up.

Picture 7: Brendan putting the play people into their box.

Picture 8: Jen putting the box on the shelf.

Picture 9: All the children together.

Picture 10: Brendan with his dad walking to the car.

Very soon Brendan was able to put the things away without having a tantrum.

Using photographs Photographs of individuals in the centre can be used to good effect to both support language and also cue children into social issues. Photos can, for instance, be placed on chairs with a No Entry sign (meaning no or not) to show that this child is not here today. Photos to show whose turn it is for something are also helpful.

Developing theory of mind All children at the pre-school stage need to develop an understanding that other people think and feel differently to them and begin to take a 'perspective of the other' into account in their interactions. Children on the autistic spectrum require extensive input.

Draw two or three people in the child's world, together with a picture of the child, in this case Aaron. There is no need for artistic skills; individuals can easily be identified by different hairstyles. Wait a moment and see if the children can offer their ideas – do not however make this a demand:

▶ *Aaron likes playing in the big car* – picture of big car with connecting line.
▶ *Bronwyn likes playing in the sand pit* – picture of sandpit and connecting line.
▶ *Mummy likes driving the car* – ditto.
▶ *Judy likes playing the guitar* – ditto.

This can develop to statements of feelings:

▶ *Aaron is angry when he can't play in the car* – picture of car with no entry sign.
▶ *Bronwyn is angry when her sandcastle gets knocked over.*
▶ *Mummy is angry when her computer goes wrong.*
▶ *Judy is angry when someone spoils a book.*

Then explore different feelings in relation to one situation.

▶ *Aaron stood on the cat's tail by accident.*
▶ *How would the cat feel?*
▶ *How would mum feel?*
▶ *How would Aaron feel?*

Do not use this exercise as a means to reprimand children, it confuses the purpose and reduces its usefulness.

Doubling, mirroring and modelling   These are other ways of helping children learn perspectives and experiment with alternative ways of being.

Doubling is a bit like parallel play – it is doing something alongside someone. Being beside the child you copy what they are doing, perhaps with simple commentary.

Mirroring is doing the same thing as the child, but this time in front of them so that they can see for themselves how they appear to others. Children may modify what they are doing when they realize this.

There are many mirroring games for young children such as 'Simon Says' where one person takes the lead in actions and others follow. Getting children to play role reversal games where they can be different characters is useful. Puppets provide another mirroring opportunity. Puppets take on characters that enable children to look at how they are playing out roles.

Modelling is not only behaving in ways that you would like children to copy but also offering alternatives to the child by acting these out. If a child is distressed, for instance, modelling deep breathing will encourage the child to copy.

Dealing with transitions Giving children warning of any changes and helping them identify and share associated feelings may pre-empt angry outbursts.

 CASE STUDY

Peter is on the autistic spectrum and has great difficulty managing transitions. Sometimes staff are not aware of what has changed in his environment to cause his distress. His key worker, however, found a way to help him by rapidly drawing a picture of a boy yelling and just saying 'scary change' to him. Initially this helped Peter to calm down more quickly and now he is able to come and say 'scary change' pointing at the picture which is on the wall.

VISUAL NARRATIVES IN RESPONSE TO CHALLENGING BEHAVIOUR

Children who cannot express their feelings in words may scream and throw tantrums instead. Visual narratives appear to provide the child with a way to feel heard. This intervention provides staff with an active response that attempts to neither restrain nor persuade the child but invariably has the effect of containment. It appears to offer a way of communicating which lessens the intensity of the interaction. All you need is a supply of paper and a willingness to tune into the child – you don't even need much in the way of drawing skills! This is not about changing behaviour but giving the child the means to communicate what is generating their distress. It also models emotional regulation and response.

This is how it works:

▶ Position yourself beside the child – do not block their exit. This is not intended to be confrontation or challenge but a support to what they are trying to communicate. What you are about to do is develop a child-driven story with a shared focus.

▶ Quickly draw the child with a clear facial expression showing the emotion being expressed.

▶ Mirror the emotion in sounds and gestures – if the child is yelling incoherently you also do this pointing at the drawing – but not necessarily as loudly!

▶ Make an educated guess about what this represents – why the child is feeling what they are feeling: what does their behaviour appear to be saying for them?

▶ Say what you think in as few words as possible, e.g. *Angry: want your turn. Anthony not finished his turn yet.*

▶ Tap your head, say to the child *You are thinking* . . . and provide a thought bubble on the drawing – repeat and write in whatever the child says – perhaps with a simple illustration, e.g *not fair – don't want to wait.* Provide children with cues if necessary – such as one of the commercially available cards showing feelings (see Chapter 4 for resources).

▶ Draw a mouth bubble and say *and you are saying* . . . – if they have enough language wait for the child to tell you – repeat and write this in with illustrations.

▶ If a child destroys the paper then simply start another one – they are damaging paper not people.

▶ When the emotions have been identified and the child has begun to calm down give them the opportunity to say what they would like to happen.

▶ The narrative can develop from this point – let it take its course. You will have a fully engaged child trying to communicate.

Teachers and others who have been using visual narratives have been surprised at how effective this has been in helping children to communicate feelings in a way that reduces difficult behaviour. Social stories then evolving from the child's own visual narratives are more likely to be effective.

Group visual narratives

Group conflicts can also be resolved using visual narratives. Sit the children in a semi-circle and start by asking *what happened first?* You then draw this on paper or a whiteboard. You develop a sequence of events with the associated feelings, identifying each child or adult involved by their hair or other distinguishing feature. You end up with an illustrated story that can be used as the basis for exploring alternative endings.

You may also like to develop this technique simply to illustrate a sequence of events of things that happen in the centre. The children will love to act this out at the end of the day.

Signing

As all young children understand language before they have the ability to speak, teaching some basic sign language has merit. It helps children communicate without words and can therefore reduce frustration and increase agency. It does not inhibit the eventual development of language but provides a useful stepping stone. Look up information about teaching babies to sign for how to go about this.

SUMMARY

Children with learning and language difficulties require expectations and responses that are at, and support, their level of functioning. Pro-actively addressing self-esteem and communication issues is likely to reduce the incidence of challenging behaviour.

Chapter 6

Healing the hurt

*Those children who have loving families but not the experiences that
foster cooperation are likely to respond well to the principles for
establishing positive behaviour given in Chapter 3. Those with learning
and communication difficulties, discussed in the previous chapter, will
account for another large percentage of the difficulties you will come
across. Yet another group of children (who may also belong to the first
two) behave in ways that are hard to manage because they have been
hurt. This may be a chronic long-term hurt with foundations in lack of
attachment, insecurity, rejection and/or abuse or acute hurt linked to
critical incidents such as family breakdown or exposure to trauma. Some
children experience both acute and chronic hurt.*

Hurt children are particularly vulnerable and needy and this makes them
demanding to work with. Struggling to get their needs met, they can
behave in ways that might quickly be labelled as spiteful, aggressive,
demanding, whinging and defiant. Seeing children as behaving this way
'deliberately' and taking this personally is not helpful in understanding,
responding to or managing challenging behaviour. Children who have
powerful reactions to damaging life experiences require more effort in
every direction and it is essential that professionals on the front line
seek both support from colleagues and ways of maintaining their
emotional resources (see Chapter 9). Accepting children but not their
behaviour is important not only for the child's self-esteem but also to
maximize their cooperation. Research indicates that children are more
likely to be compliant when approval is high but follow directives less
willingly when approval is low (Atwater and Morris 1988).

It is worth remembering that we cannot change a child's history, experiences or circumstances. We can only change what we think, say and do in the hopes of the best outcomes. If we work as constructively as possible with both the child and their family, using all our knowledge, skills, sensitivity and emotional intelligence, we stand a good chance of making a difference within the boundaries of what is possible. Even if we cannot heal the hurt we can offer comfort and secure boundaries. These include clear and consistent expectations for behaviour. Compassion for children who have been hurt does not mean tolerating behaviour that is hurtful. It gives messages that such behaviour is acceptable. We can provide a safe environment and a positive relationship. We can also model caring, coping and problem-solving. There are strong links between this chapter and Chapter 4.

It is common in many early years centres for all children to have a 'key worker' attached to them. If this is not the case in your centre consider having a key worker for each child who requires a high level of support. Although responsibilities should be shared it is helpful to have someone establish a special relationship with the child and their family throughout their time in the pre-school environment. Louise Porter (2003) suggests several escalating ways a key worker might support a child who is displaying distressed behaviour:

▶ Changing the expectation/activity so that it is less demanding for the child.
▶ Participating in activities with the child to help scaffold learning, especially social and emotional learning.
▶ 'Shadowing' where the child accompanies the key worker in their activities until he is feeling less 'out of control' and is able to rejoin the group. This is not a punishment but to provide support.

WHAT HURTS?

There have been volumes written about the following issues. This chapter can only touch on what are complex and challenging situations. It is important to remember that each child and each situation is individual. Responses will depend on many variables. What follows is for general guidance.

Poor attachment

Attachment is the bond between a carer and infant that provides emotional nurturance. This nurturance includes responding readily and sensitively to the baby's communication, feeding them when they are hungry, comforting them when they are distressed, smiling back at them, being available. There is increasing scientific evidence that a lack of attachment in infancy, and the resulting interaction of physiology and psychology, has potentially far-reaching implications for the child and their development (Gerhardt 2004). When parents are either lacking in response or hostile, fear and stress levels in babies go up, cortisol levels increase and they become both demanding and more difficult to comfort. Over time, infants appear to cope with this insecurity by shutting out feelings. Babies who have their dependency needs denied grow up with poor self-awareness and therefore do not develop good emotional regulation. They become either clingy and demanding or defensive/aggressive – or alternate between the two. Unsurprisingly, they have more difficulty developing empathy. Bowlby (1973) sums up the poorly attached child's perception of the world as 'comfortless and unpredictable' and responses to this world as 'shrinking from it or doing battle with it'. Maternal depression also appears to impact on biochemical structures in the developing infant brain, which reduces the capacity for positive emotionality (Depue *et al.* 1994).

What this means in the pre-school environment is children who find it hard to relate to others, have poor self-worth, high levels of anxiety and attention needs and a tendency to focus on the negative. You cannot provide a pre-schooler with a new start but there are a number of things that early years educators might do to minimize the impact of poor attachment:

- ▶ acknowledge and validate any feelings the child may be expressing;
- ▶ talk about feelings, give the child words for emotions, encourage self-awareness;
- ▶ help children to identify positives;
- ▶ when children indicate fear or insecurity show them that there are people in the centre who will take care of them;
- ▶ show warmth and affection;
- ▶ provide predictability and consistency;

95

▶ be tolerant of attention needs and recognize them as determined by fear (Geddes 2003);

▶ help with emotional regulation (see Chapter 4);

▶ help the child have a sense of agency – that they can impact on their world, give them choices, elicit their views and listen to what they have to say;

▶ show them that consideration for others will also meet their needs;

▶ always refer to *behaviour* as unacceptable while reinforcing your acceptance of them;

▶ help children identify what comforts them;

▶ model responsive relationships;

▶ work in collaboration with parents (see Chapter 7) to raise their confidence and understanding of their child's needs, keeping in mind that emotional support to families provides indirect emotional support to children.

 CASE STUDY

One primary school has designed a special place for their troubled young students. This is a foam cocoon structure filled with soft cushions and quiet music where children can choose to go if they are agitated. This is the children's choice, not used as a 'time-out' sanction.

Loss

Loss can be an under-recognized issue for pre-school children. There appears to be a conceptualization that small children cannot conceive of loss and that it doesn't impinge on them. Nothing can be further from the truth. Brown (1999) outlines four stages of grief which may be displayed in children's behaviour: anxiety, anger, denial and sadness. These responses need to be understood by adults and opportunities provided to express these feelings safely. Help to move through emotions rather than deny them will result in less damaging behaviours. Behaviour related primarily to loss will be out of character with a child's previous behaviour so it is important to identify what has changed in the child's world.

Strong responses to loss are evident where children lose significant people in their lives. As well as death and family breakdown, sometimes family members serve a term of imprisonment, are in hospital or have long periods working away from home. The impact of the loss may be exacerbated by the possibility that remaining carers may be overwhelmed by their own distress and therefore emotionally unavailable for a while (Dowling and Gorell Barnes 2000). It is also made worse if the child is a pawn in a continuing parental battle after separation or if promises are made about access that are not kept. Because of the egocentricity connected to their conceptual understanding children of this age often believe that they are responsible in some way for the loss.

 CASE STUDY

Five-year-old Leo was constantly in trouble for defiance in the class-room and aggression in the playground. His mum, Robyn, said that he was as good as gold at home and she couldn't understand it. A conversation revealed that Leo's dad had left home six months earlier and no-one had talked to him about this. Robyn had also been very upset and did not realize the impact this family disruption would have on her son. When the psychologist met with Leo his eyes filled with tears as he told her: 'I am a bad boy, my daddy left so I must be bad.' Robyn was encouraged to talk with Leo and reassure him that it was not his fault and that she was not going to leave him too. Leo's difficult behaviour began to improve almost immediately.

Pre-schoolers do not appreciate permanence and may fantasize that life will return to the way it was before. For this reason, sometimes children behave as if the loss is not important, especially at first. Some adults find these responses callous or disturbing, rather than within developmental expectations. They may also be reassured that the child is coping well and be surprised when faced with later difficulties. If there has been a bereavement this needs to be explained in straight-forward language – saying that someone has 'gone to sleep' may cause problems at bedtime.

In the early years setting:

▶ Be aware of sudden changes in behaviour and investigate further if possible.
▶ Expect some regression and increased dependence.
▶ Provide information at a level the child can understand – or encourage and help parents to do so. This should include reassurance that the child was not responsible for any loss.
▶ Reassure children of ongoing stability in as many areas of their lives as possible.
▶ Acknowledge and validate emotions, offer comfort when appropriate.
▶ Provide opportunities to work through difficult feelings through play and discussion. There are now excellent books available for young children that deal with these issues.
▶ Be aware of psychosomatic complaints – tummy aches, etc.
▶ Help parents to appreciate how their child might conceptualize the loss as a pre-schooler and how this is different from adult understanding.

Losses do not have to be major in adult terms for them to impact significantly on children (see the Case Study on p. 99).

Trauma

Trauma is any major event that is out of the norm that causes stress to the person involved. It can be anything from actually being in or witnessing a serious accident, natural disaster or violent crime to the fear initiated by a burglary or someone brandishing a weapon. Some children will have been traumatized by being in civil war zones, others by violence at home. Young children are particularly vulnerable because of their high level of dependence on caregivers who may be involved and because they do not have the cognition or language to help them understand what has happened.

The impact of trauma varies depending on the circumstances. It is more severe if the people involved are significant to the child and the trauma is not an isolated incident. It is mediated if there is family and community support with individual coping mechanisms already in place. The coping strategies of others will have a significant impact on how well the child recovers.

CASE STUDY

Femi was four and had been coming to the centre three days a week for two months. This was her third placement in two years. Both parents were locum doctors, moving around for work. Femi's father was in Nigeria on a six-month placement. Although Femi settled well, enjoying a range of activities in the centre, she often asked for her mother during the day, becoming tearful before her mother picked her up at around 5.30. If she was late Femi became inconsolable. Staff were also concerned that Femi sought adult company rather than interacting with other children. She asked for help she did not really need, asked questions when she already knew the answer and followed a certain member of staff around. Femi became distressed when this staff member went for her break or was away for the day. Following further discussions the following strategies were agreed:

► Femi's key worker explained the need to be on time and asked Femi's mother to let the setting know if this was unavoidable. It was suggested that Femi always know where Mum and Dad are and that when Dad is away he makes regular contact. The family were asked to communicate any likely changes so staff could reassure Femi.

► Femi's key worker made a 'routine' book with Femi with pictures and photographs of her day. It covered days at the centre and at home and included all the key people in her life. This was used to encourage conversation about routines and to help Femi with transitions or when she was distressed.

► Femi was encouraged to work with an adult plus one child, then two children, then larger groups of children using activities she enjoys.

► An additional key worker was identified to address the issue of staff absence.

► All staff were asked to praise Femi for independence.

At a review just before she transferred to school, Femi's key worker reported that she was much less distressed, more confident and independent. She had made friends with two children who were transferring to the same Primary School. Her parents were both now settled in permanent jobs.

In pre-school settings post-traumatic effects can include:

► increased fragmentation and poor concentration;
► hyper-vigilance and anxiety;
► tiredness caused by fear of falling asleep and having nightmares;
► regression;
► increased dependence;
► 'acting out' in play scenarios;
► preoccupation with details of the event;
► 'withdrawn' behaviour;
► unexpected fears triggered by sights, smells and sounds.

Early years professionals are better placed to manage more challenging behaviour if they know what has happened. There are circumstances, however, when that information will not be available. The most effective ways of responding are:

► No expectation that there will be a rapid resolution.
► Respect the child's fears: *I know you may be feeling frightened. I wonder what we could do so you are not so frightened.* Seeing adults taking these fears seriously but not being overwhelmed by them is reassuring. There should be no expectations that the child will be 'tough' or 'brave' but expectations that they will feel better in time.
► Help the child identify what comforts them when they are distressed. Having a 'transition object' from home such as a blanket or teddy is often helpful. This should be freely available in the early years setting.
► A safe place or person to go to: if the family is in turmoil help them agree for someone to act as a 'buffer' for the child. Grandparents and aunts in particular can make all the difference in providing a secure and responsive relationship.
► Good models of emotional management.
► Comfort to relieve bodily tension, rocking, soothing music. The child may need frequent physical holding and cuddles – who is best to provide this?
► Talk about the here and now, especially when the child appears to be experiencing flashbacks – and confirm the safety of their present environment.
► Tolerate frequent re-telling of the event or no ability to talk about it at all.

▶ Make provision for play and provide small toys as appropriate, such as ambulances, etc. Adults may find it hard to listen to but being able to act out symbolically helps with the healing process. It gives children imaginative control in a situation in which they experienced helplessness.

▶ Do, however, intervene where play is aggressive towards other children, is sexualized or where the individual constantly places themselves as victim.

Abuse

Children who are abused have suffered trauma and may display many of the behaviours described above. Abuse, whether physical, sexual or psychological, is usually perpetrated by those who are supposed to care for and protect the child. This makes the trauma doubly disorienting and damaging. Sexual abuse, marked by threats, betrayal of trust, violence and pain is a severe psychological assault.

Children who are abused may:

▶ not respond positively to friendly overtures;
▶ not seek comfort;
▶ not be interested in play or exploration;
▶ expect to be treated badly and even provoke this;
▶ show little emotion or have poor emotional regulation;
▶ be aggressive;
▶ have difficulty focusing on activities;
▶ be impulsive;
▶ seek close contact with adults/be clingy;
▶ have sexual knowledge which is developmentally inappropriate;
▶ touch themselves and/or others inappropriately;
▶ have delayed development compared to their peers;
▶ exhibit none of the above – signs of abuse are not always obvious.

Early years staff need to know what the regulations about mandatory reporting are. If you are unsure about evidence of abuse keep a log book and monitor incidents over time.

The following applies to all children but is particularly important for responding to those who have been abused:

▶ See the child as someone with strengths and individuality rather than as a victim.

▶ Comment on their strengths, abilities and achievements.

▶ Do not overwhelm the child in any way – they may not be able to respond to friendly overtures. Be subtle, gentle, consistent and positive in your approach.

▶ Help children recognize their feelings and know when they don't feel safe.

▶ Provide all children in your centre with a 'personal safety' training programme.

▶ Work with carers to change the culture of 'secret'. This is a powerful notion for young children. Introduce 'surprise' or 'waiting to tell/show something special' as alternatives.

▶ Give children strategies to use in circumstances where safety is threatened. Shouting and screaming is sometimes an appropriate thing to do.

▶ Support friendship development – children who have been rejected are often very sensitive and react strongly to perceived rejection – or they do the rejecting first. Early years educators need to be aware of this so they can actively intervene.

Get specific training – this is a complex and emotionally confronting issue for professionals.

Inappropriate expectations

Children can be hurt by well-meaning adults without them realizing. Most of this is related to poor understanding of a child's needs and development in the early years. It may also be related to a desire for children to meet the parents' need for status. Adults who try to fit a child to their expectations rather than their expectations to the child are in danger of damaging that child's real potential.

It is valuable for parents to understand the rationale of activities that take place in the early years centre. Information on how social and emotional development is an essential aspect of academic learning may also help.

CASE STUDY

Amina is a very able four-year-old. She developed language early, has an excellent memory and enjoys problem-solving activities. She was, however, becoming increasingly agitated in the centre – her concentration was beginning to become fragmented and her creativity less marked. The reasons became clear when her father came to talk to the head of the centre. He was not happy that Amina was spending her time 'playing' and wanted her to be accelerated into 'real school' as soon as possible. He asserted that his daughter was 'going to be a Nobel Prize winner one day'. Amina's mother confided that her daughter was subjected to 'number exercises' every evening and was ceasing to be the lively, curious child she once had been.

Children who have had inappropriate expectations put on them may be highly sensitive to 'not getting things right' and be reluctant to explore their environment for fear of getting into trouble. They need:

▶ to feel that mistakes are part of learning;
▶ opportunities for creative play;
▶ to have their strengths celebrated;
▶ encouragement to interact with peers in fun activities;
▶ experience of an adult who accepts who they are.

SUMMARY

Hurt children often behave in ways that challenge educators. It is essential that we work collaboratively to support each other to respond with a high level of professional integrity. Many early years practitioners are understandably concerned about behaviours that impede harmony in the setting (Papatheodorou 2000) but when pre-schoolers are 'excluded' from an educational placement serious questions must be asked about what we mean by inclusive practices. Rejecting an already vulnerable young child has significant impact on both the child and their family. The following chapter will help early years professionals explore ways of managing specific difficulties that also focus on meeting longer-term needs.

Chapter 7

Behaviours that challenge

Even the most experienced practitioner is occasionally unsure about the best way to deal with a specific behaviour. This chapter offers a response framework that helps with immediate management while bearing in mind the longer-term needs of the child. It is not intended to be prescriptive as each child and each context is different. This chapter builds on what has already gone before in establishing pro-social behaviours within an emotionally safe environment. Success of the strategies below depends on the context in which they are embedded. It is not just what you do that matters, but how you do it.

If a behaviour is of concern you need to look at what else the child is doing or not doing in order to build up a full picture of learning, language, developmental and psychological needs. Keep dated records detailing what the centre has put in place. This includes liaison with families and how any individual plan has been monitored and reviewed. This will inform conversations with other professionals and any future special needs assessment.

RESPONDING TO HIGH LEVELS OF EMOTION IN CHILDREN

In Chapter 3 we looked at the many 'C' words involved in establishing and maintaining pro-social behaviour. Here are more 'C' words that are useful in responding to a high level of expressed emotion, whether this is anger, fear or other distress.

Sometimes the emotion is expressed quite mildly at first but becomes 'louder' if this is not recognized. In other situations overwhelming feelings seem to swamp young children. Early years educators need to help them recover from an emotional overload and take back some control before attempting any other intervention.

Consider feelings first

You might be angry or tearful about something and go to your partner or close friend to tell them about it. Often the other person, worried for you and wanting to 'make it better', goes into problem-solving mode and starts suggesting how things might be resolved. But what you want is to offload, have someone listen and acknowledge that you are just feeling grim. You are not ready for good advice, however well intentioned.

It is useful to think of this with children. Not paying enough attention to feelings may mean that behavioural difficulties are exacerbated as the child does increasingly 'loud' things in order to be 'heard'. Reflecting back to children what they are feeling can be both validating and reassuring which will calm them down. It also models a language for emotions.

 CASE STUDY

After several months of being quite happy coming to the nursery class three days a week, three-year-old Abbey started to cry when her mother, Zoë, left to go to work. There had been no change of personnel and no new children in the centre – and she was cheerful again half an hour after her mother had left. The extent of her sobbing, however, was distressing for everyone, especially Zoë who had done everything she could think of to reassure her daughter and say she would be 'all right'. One day, in desperation, she gently said to Abbey 'I know you don't want me to go but I have to. I can see that you are very sad. Perhaps you should just have a good cry until the sadness goes away and you are ready to join in'. The crying stopped within two days.

Being exposed to distress is unsettling and it is natural to want to cheer people up – but this may be more for our benefit than the one who is hurting.

Stay calm

Being calm is easier said than done when a child's behaviour is hurtful, defiant or they are having a tantrum. Children, especially young ones, however, both refer to and mirror the emotional state of the adults around them. If adults are fearful or angry then the child is more likely to be. If adults are calm and in control of themselves and the situation, children will calm down sooner.

When faced with a challenging situation, you can stay calm on the outside if you remember the following:

▶ keep your voice low and slow (children hear the volume, tenor and pitch much more easily than they hear the words);

▶ breath deeply and evenly;

▶ be at the child's level to ensure that your calm presence is fully evident;

▶ do not invade the child's space by finger pointing or thrusting your face forward;

▶ try to avoid an angry expression.

Concern not interrogation

Being calm does not mean being bland. Children need to know that what they do matters to significant people. It is important the child recognizes that you are concerned about them: *I am unhappy that you are having such a bad day today.*

Don't try and get to the bottom of things if the child is in a state. Asking 'why?' is rarely useful. Even adults are not always aware of the multiple and complex reasons for their actions, although they may be able to tell you about the final trigger. When the child has calmed down a little, you will get a better picture if you ask: *What were you thinking when you did that?* or *What did you want to happen?* If the child is able to answer, this may help in understanding the perceptions and judgements that gave rise to the feelings underpinning their behaviour. Feelings may be buried in deep emotional memory, however, giving rise to negative thoughts rather than the other way round (Goleman 1996).

Coping

Convey faith in the child's ability to cope with a difficult situation. If they are having a tantrum, rather than tell them to stop this – which is unlikely to have much of an impact – try reassurance instead. Tell them firmly and gently: *It is OK, you will be OK, you will be able to calm down, you will be feeling better soon, you know what to do, take a deep breath like this.* A narrative approach may help: *You just tell that screaming voice to get lost: come on, you can do it.*

Telling children how bad they are at the height of an emotional outburst is not helpful. Discussing with them afterwards about what they could have done instead is a better idea.

Comfort

The child may initially feel distressed, not only by the triggering incident, but also by losing control. Offer the child some physical comfort when they begin to calm down. Help them identify what comforts them. Even if you want to address the more unacceptable behaviours this will ease the transition into a conversation.

Adults also need to know what comforts them when they have dealt with high levels of emotion.

Care

Adults need to disapprove of behaviour while showing acceptance of the child, e.g.: *Tearing up Marlon's painting has really upset him. That was unkind. You know how to be a kind person. I have seen you do it. What do you think you might do to make things better for Marlon. If it was your painting that was torn what might make you feel better?* If the adult demonstrates care they are reinforcing the significant relationship that is central to the child's ability to respond positively.

Compassion

All of the above demonstrates and models compassion. It is important that hurting others is addressed with strong disapproval – especially for children who have been hurt. It gives constant messages that such behaviours are not acceptable while responding in ways that do not exacerbate the damage for anyone.

Summary: The 'C' words in responding to a high level of emotion

Consider feelings first: sometimes children just need to be heard.

Stay **calm**: children will mirror the emotion expressed.

Show **concern**: being calm does not mean being bland, children need to know that what they do matters to you.

Coping: convey belief in the child's ability to recover control.

Comfort: identify what comforts the child.

Care: disapprove of the behaviour, while showing acceptance of the child.

Compassion: it is important that children know that hurting others is not acceptable.

Temper tantrums

The most common 'high level of emotion' that early years educators have to deal with is that displayed in tantrums. Most two- and three-year-olds have occasional tantrums, especially before there is sufficient language to express needs and feelings. Tantrums should only be a cause of concern if they are excessive and/or not lessening as children get nearer school age. They are usually triggered by frustration when desires or expectations are thwarted. Young children often want things to be 'just right' and get distraught when they are not, even though this may seem unreasonable or trivial to an adult. The child becomes overwhelmed by their feelings and needs support to recover control. Tantrums are more likely to happen when children are tired, unwell or hungry.

Taking evasive action such as awareness of physical needs, giving children warning of what is about to happen or giving them limited choices helps limit tantrums (see negotiation in Chapter 2). When they do occur they are best dealt with in line with the guidance above, e.g. as calmly as possible – not always easy! – acknowledging feelings and encouraging the use of words.

Dealing with tantrums often comes down to a battle for control. Aiming for 'win/win' outcomes takes more effort but provides a more effective learning experience. Offering the child some limited control without 'giving in' to demands helps promote a sense of agency without reinforcing the behaviour: *I know you are upset that Jack is wearing the Superman outfit and you wanted it. You can't have it now but would you like to have it later or choose another outfit now instead?*

Be reassuring and tell children they will be OK again soon. If the child is doing something dangerous intervene – but say what you are doing as you are doing it. Sometimes it is useful for children to be gently removed from the situation to calm down. This gives the message that the tantrum is unacceptable in company but also acknowledges distress. Give the child the option to rejoin others when they are feeling more 'in control of themselves' again. Give positive feedback and comfort as soon as the intensity lessens. Talk through alternatives later.

Where children are having difficulty expressing themselves in words and resort to vocal and physical communications try the visual narratives described in Chapter 5.

SPECIFIC BEHAVIOURS

We now deal with a range of the specific behaviours that may occur in the pre-school setting that are particularly challenging for early years staff. Not all behaviours of concern are addressed here but some of the strategies are adaptable to other situations. There are several components to be addressed for each of these:

▶ Assessment: What can you do to find out more? This would include a conversation with parents as outlined in Chapter 8. It is useful to identify competencies and contextual factors. This helps with knowing where and how to plan an intervention.

▶ Prevention: Action you might take to prevent or limit the behaviour.

▶ Management: What you might do when it is occurring. It is important that immediate management strategies are congruent with maintaining positive relationships and meeting longer-term needs. This includes ensuring that the centre is a safe environment for everyone.

▶ Needs: How you might meet the child's needs in the longer term and what you could do to promote change.

See the Individual Behaviour Plan at the end of this chapter.

Biting

Most children go through a biting stage but this is usually over by three years. It is more often a response to frustration rather than an indication of deep distress. Whatever the motivation, biting is unacceptable because of the hurt to other children.

Assessment   Is there a pattern to the behaviour? When does it happen most/least? What are the triggers? Is biting one of a number of worrying behaviours or does it stand alone? What are parents' responses?

Prevention   When you know the flash points for the behaviour then you can intervene. Give the children 'scripts' to help them use words to express themselves. You may also find it useful to give children something to bite on. Other children benefit from taking assertive action to prevent or limit any hurtful behaviour. Teach them to put up their hands in front of them and say loudly 'No, I don't like it'.

Management   Immediately remove the child, saying: *Biting hurts. You are not allowed to hurt your friends and other people here are not allowed to hurt you.* Give attention to the child who has been bitten but the biter needs to take responsibility for helping look after them, washing wounds and putting on plasters. The seriousness of biting needs to be reinforced as it makes the centre unsafe.

Meeting longer-term needs   Conversations need to be around feelings and what words could be used instead of biting. Help children to recognize a developing impulse and take evasive action – perhaps biting on an object chosen by the child for this purpose.

NB: Occasionally, biting, smelling, licking, spinning and hand flapping are behaviours that indicate the child has autistic tendencies. You need to check whether there are other behaviours of concern such as strong fear of change, repetitive/obsessive behaviours, little evidence of symbolic play and very poor social skills. If this is the case then you will require specialist advice. Be very wary, however, of jumping to conclusions. One symptom does not make a syndrome.

Defiance

We might not like it but young children are supposed to be sometimes defiant rather than always compliant! It is part of their developing independence and individuality. Along with defiance, however, is also a desire to please significant people and a developmental pathway to cooperation and collaboration. It is these that we should be addressing and encouraging.

Assessment   When and with whom is the child most willing to cooperate? Are there patterns to the defiance and is this in response to what is being specifically asked? What works in persuading the child to cooperate? Are you sure that the child can hear and understand you?

Prevention   Giving limited choices rather than insisting 'do it now' gives the child some control in the situation. Giving warning of transitions also helps. Check that the requests being made of the child are within their ability, make sense to them and in some way meet their needs. Explain briefly why you are asking for compliance. The way you phrase a request matters. Direct orders are less likely to be received well. Making too many demands or making these when a child is otherwise not able to comply – such as when they are overtired or distressed – increases the chance of defiance.

Management   It saves emotional energy if you avoid a power struggle. Give the child some time to comply if possible and move away from the situation. Try and stay light-hearted and offer a natural consequence, phrased positively where possible: *If you clear up soon, you will be ready when your mummy arrives.* If necessary help with the activity so that you can commend the child for cooperating – however minimally.

Meeting longer-term needs   A child who is frequently defiant may be angry and perhaps used to power struggles. Developing a supportive relationship raises the motivation to be cooperative.

Destructive, damaging outbursts

This refers to all those behaviours that hurt others or are destructive of property. Children who punch, spit, kick, pull hair or throw things are avoided by their peers and will spend much time alone. The same applies to those who scribble on other children's pictures and knock down constructions. There often appears to be a cycle of behaviour in which children reject before they are rejected. Children who are aggressive towards others are usually angry because of something that has happened to them and often very unhappy. Supportive intervention is required to reverse the negative spiral. Some children may not have age-appropriate social awareness of others, which requires a developmental investigation.

Assessment   What patterns are evident in the outbursts? Can you identify contributory contextual factors? Is it recent or ongoing? What does the child appear to be communicating by this behaviour? Does the child have poor language skills? What is his response to intervention/ sanctions or retaliation? Does he seek attention by this behaviour? What does the family say about what happens at home and how do they respond? Have any interventions been successful and in which ways? Is this part of a pattern of other behaviours that are of concern?

Prevention   Group cohesion reduces aggression (Farver 1996). Circle time and friendship activities are useful as they encourage social skills and reduce rejection. Children need encouragement to 'use your words' to express feelings and needs. Give positive attention and reinforcement when the child does do this – even if they are yelling! Ensure that other children are also given strategies to limit such behaviour (see 'Biting' on p. 110).

Management   Ask the child to stop what they are doing now and give them an action to comply with: *Chris, come here.* Doing something is easier than stopping something. Intervene if they do not respond. This is not the moment for giving 'chances'. Say that you can see that he is upset but state strongly that the child is not allowed to hurt others and others are not allowed to hurt him. Ensure that you separate the child from the behaviour in order to maintain relationships, using 'I statements'. Comfort the child who has been hurt in the presence of the perpetrator. Asking children to 'do sorry' helps them realize there are consequences to their behaviour and they are responsible. Do not, however, insist if this will provoke another confrontation. Instead model empathy and concern.

Meeting longer-term needs   Children need to know that this behaviour is strongly disapproved of by people that matter to them. Adults need to demonstrate serious disappointment but also show belief in the child to change. Children who are regularly violent towards their peers need a restricted context so that they can build more appropriate behaviours and do not put the safe environment at risk for others. This might mean having them in small supervised groups for limited periods and building on this. Close, supportive relationships with parents and ongoing assessment will also help clarify needs and appropriate interventions. The suggestions for developing emotional regulation in Chapter 4 are also relevant here.

Fragmented attention/restlessness

Young children tend not to stay with one activity for long and need constant variety. They may be able to concentrate well but for short periods. It may be inappropriate to expect young children to sit still and focus for any length of time, especially in a passive group activity. There is some evidence that early years educators over-estimate young children's ability to do this (Katz 1995). Children who cannot hold their attention for more than a few moments in any situation, however, need help. Children who are anxious may also have this difficulty.

Assessment   Where and when is the child's attention most focused? What supports their concentration? Is poor attention causing difficulties in other ways – such as peer interaction? Is the child anxious about anything in particular?

Prevention   Identifying distractions may enable you to reduce these. Raise awareness for the child that they can concentrate in some circumstances and give them acknowledgement and the foundations of a self-concept as 'someone who can'. If their difficulties are most apparent when they are expected to sit in a group and listen to an adult, limit this and/or have them close to you so you can support their engagement. Address anxieties where possible.

Management   You will extend concentration if you do something *with* the child. Give targets such as building a tower 'so high' or doing a painting in three colours – then extend the goal. Sometimes providing restless children with something to fiddle with is helpful.

Meeting longer-term needs   Children may not appreciate that activities have a beginning, middle and end. Reinforce this concept with them and also with parents. TV programmes, stories in books, mealtimes can all be used to emphasize this concept. Children need to begin to see themselves as people who are able to 'finish' something so success must be built into any programme. Children may also respond to 'soothing' activities such as cranial massage.

There is considerable debate about attention deficit hyperactivity disorder and the potential for over-diagnosis. Sometimes children are reacting to events in their lives or are very lively children who find it hard to meet expectations for staying still. Some families choose to medicate their child to improve their attention. It is worth trying the above and checking whether diet is exacerbating the problem before taking this step.

Impulsiveness

This often goes with fragmented attention. It takes significant energy for a small child to stop themselves doing something they want to do. The increase in self-control between the ages of two and five depends on many things. Brain maturity needs to reach the point where it is possible to acknowledge that a decision has to be made and language skills used in self-talk are sufficiently developed. Whether or not the child is able to check their impulses at any given time will also depend on context, such as how tired they are or whether there are additional 'control' factors such as a significant adult in the vicinity.

Assessment Check language skills and other learning issues. Is the impulsive behaviour generic or specific? The child's age is an important factor. If the child is four and there is still a marked lack of control the child needs support to develop this.

Prevention Risk assessment. Ensure that safety for the child and others is maximized. Be very clear about expectations (see Chapter 3). The internal voice of control for the child is initially yours. The more significant the relationship the more likely the voice will be in the child's mind to restrain the impulse. Work with the child to recognize how they are constantly making decisions and can choose to do or not do things. Offer choices to reinforce this.

Management When the child has acted on impulse they need:

► to be aware of what their actions have caused so that they learn cause and effect;

► to identify the choices in the situation;

▶ to be asked what they should have done (not be told – the aim is to develop thinking);

▶ to take some responsibility for making amends – 'doing sorry' rather than just 'saying sorry'.

Meeting longer-term needs The natural development of impulse control is enhanced by language skills, which enable the child to have the internal dialogue necessary for self-control. Children also benefit from opportunities to take some responsibility. Start small with what the child can manage and give positive reinforcement for success (and help where necessary). A child who is told 'you can't be trusted with that' will not learn how to be. Acknowledge when a child is able to restrain impulse.

Blaming others

This is a demonstration of the realization that what has happened is not acceptable and that the impulses got the better of the restraint – see it as a move in the right direction and do not get too upset about it. Let the child know that you are aware that they are responsible. Model acceptance of making mistakes yourself and show the child that they are not expected to get everything right all the time: no one does.

Not speaking (selective mutism)

This is where language is at the expected stage of development at home but the child does not speak in the early years setting. This is usually related to anxiety and lack of confidence or the child is very shy.

Assessment What language and social skills does the child have at home? How is she communicating non-verbally in the centre, if at all? What peer group interactions does she have? What is the most useful point from which to build an intervention?

Prevention Families may reduce anxiety in their shy children by giving positive messages about the early years centre – it may also help if the child has a known 'friend' to be with.

Management Responses need to develop confidence and reduce anxiety so positioning the child as stubborn and being cross or insistent are counter-productive. Give the child a way of indicating needs visually and show that you believe she will speak when she is ready.

Meeting longer-term needs   Build confidence by providing opportunities to contribute non-verbally. Close home–school collaboration will help, such as inviting family members into the pre-school setting or inviting other children home.

 CASE STUDY

Natasha M. speaks both English and Chinese at home and although has good social skills is very shy. She did not speak from the moment she set foot in school, not even to ask to go to the toilet. Her teacher at first thought Natasha was stubborn but after talking with the school counsellor realised that anxiety was preventing her from communicating.

Natasha was told she did not have to speak until she was ready and that everyone was going to help her. She was given picture cards on her desk to initiate communication with the teacher, such as to ask for the toilet or to have a drink. Natasha was encouraged to raise her hand then point to the card. She received incremental rewards for this. On three mornings a week Natasha's mother went into the classroom with her before anyone was there. Mrs M. asked Natasha to show her things and encouraged her to talk about them. The teacher made a tape talking about a book and asking questions with gaps for Natasha to answer. Natasha is practising the answers at home and when she is ready will record the answers. With Natasha's agreement the tape will be played in class so the other children can hear her voice.

Natasha has responded well to the programme so far and is making slow but steady progress. She is mouthing words to her teacher and interactions with peers have improved significantly. Everyone is very pleased.

Self-stimulation

This is where children consistently touch and rub their genital region in public. This behaviour is not uncommon in pre-school children but often disturbing to early years staff and may attract attention from other parents. It is important not to jump to conclusions about what is causing this. If abuse is a concern other behaviours will support this hypothesis. The behaviour may be related to feeling sore in that region or simply the discovery of a comfort strategy. It is the public display that needs addressing.

Assessment Discuss concerns with parents and whether they have noticed similar behaviour. Has there been a medical check? Are there times it is more likely to happen, such as when the child is sleepy?

Prevention Distractions, a comfort object and/or giving the child something else to do with their hands might help.

Management   Ignore rather than draw attention to this if it occurs in a group setting. If an awareness programme has begun, remind the child privately that this is not the place. You may also agree a private sign with the child.

Meeting longer-term needs The child needs to know that this behaviour itself is not wrong but is something for a private place. It is also worth monitoring for associated indications of a more serious concern.

Toileting issues

All young children have occasional accidents but this refers to children over the age of three who wet or soil themselves regularly. This is more likely to happen where there are associated developmental difficulties but will also happen when children have been distressed by events in their lives.

Assessment There may be medical reasons for frequent toileting mishaps. Is this a recent phenomenon or has the child never learnt to be clean and dry? If it is recent then it may be indicative of some psychological distress. Check out with parents any medical investigations and/or recent changes in the child's life. It may also be useful to identify any patterns in the behaviour. Does the child know when they have a full bowel or bladder? Can they indicate they need to go to the toilet? Do they get so absorbed in activities they leave it too late?

Prevention   Toileting the child at regular intervals may help. Help them to recognize the signals that they need to go. For children who get absorbed watch out for the jiggling and direct them!

Management   It is the assault on self-esteem that requires attention. Be discreet in cleaning up. Where this is happening frequently it may be appropriate to put the child in trainer pants while other options are explored.

Meeting longer-term needs   This will depend on the assessment. Structured programmes to maximize the control possible must begin from the child's level of awareness/ability. If they are distressed it is important to shield them from further upset.

Some children play with their excrement or smear it. This may be linked to more serious learning difficulties or control issues. Sometimes children behave as if the only things they can control are what goes in or out of their bodies. These children need a greater sense of agency and to be offered choices.

Unskilled social behaviour

In the early years environment children need to share toys, equipment and attention. They have to learn to take turns and develop cooperative play skills. For some children this does not come easily. Behaviour that could be labelled as selfish and domineering is more appropriately described as unskilled and at an earlier stage of learning.

Assessment   What can the child already do in social situations? In which ways does she interact with her peers, take initiatives and communicate? Does she understand the need for basic rules for games? In which circumstances is she able to share? Does she recognize and acknowledge when others share with her? Are social difficulties part of a wider difficulty or do they stand alone?

Prevention   Where possible have enough to go round so that children only have to share a limited amount. Otherwise you will have stressful scenarios all day. Many activities in the centre provide opportunities for taking turns. Regular discussions about these concepts will help, as will visual indicators for turn-taking. Be aware that children who have experienced loss may find it harder to share and may even take things from others. Avoid being judgemental and talk through feelings. Talk with children about how they join in games and what makes games good fun. Games need few, simple rules made clear at the outset. Comments on and models for positive social interactions help children learn what works.

Management   Support children with social difficulties in social situations. This may mean an adult playing a turn-taking game with them first, then inviting one other child and so on. An eggtimer or alarm clock may help structure turn-taking and is seen to be fair. When social conflicts appear to be developing verbalize what is happening and ask children to problem-solve, providing guidance where necessary.

Meeting longer-term needs   The work of the early years practitioner is to foster the motivation to collaborate and promote the development of social competence so that children can enjoy the benefits of positive peer interaction. Remember that small children have a conceptual understanding of friendship that does not yet include reciprocity. A friend is someone who plays with you and invites you to their party! Whole group activities such as circle-time games help develop skills for everyone. Individual programmes need to be embedded in social situations rather than provided for individuals (Roffey *et al.* 1994).

SUMMARY

The approaches here have their foundations in the preceding chapters. Relationships and ethos are both crucial. Some children need more intensive and structured support to develop pro-social behaviours. When appropriate strategies are put into place consistently within a supportive context and monitored and amended over time behaviour is likely to improve. Where it does not, you need to look at the broader picture and seek advice. It is useful to have well documented individual education plans to inform discussions and further assessment. The Individual Behaviour Plan given on p. 120 is intended to provide flexible guidelines for intervention so that early years educators can develop a deeper understanding of the child and their needs through a 'do and review' process.

It is helpful in all circumstances for both practitioners and parents to identify and acknowledge steps in the right direction rather than only focus on what is still not right. This maintains hopefulness instead of despair in challenging situations.

PROFORMA FOR AN INDIVIDUAL BEHAVIOUR PLAN

This is to be developed by early years educators in collaboration with caregivers.

Name:

Age:

Date:

Part A: Information to be taken into account in developing Parts B and C

Is this a new plan or a revised plan? If revised what are the outcomes of previous plans and how do they inform this one?

What is currently of most concern and to whom?

What has met with a measure of success and might be built upon?

Child strengths and qualities

Learning, language and/or other needs

Relationships

Contextual needs or circumstances, including family issues and centre resources

What will caregivers and key workers need to support their intervention?

Any other relevant information

MANAGEMENT AND LEARNING PLAN

PART B: Management plan

What will happen when the child's behaviour requires intervention?

Step 1

Step 2

Step 3

PART C: Meeting longer-term needs

What is the current overall aim? What does the child need to learn/develop/experience?

Where is the child in relation to this aim? Which factors enhance a positive outcome?

What is the specific focus for this intervention? What will demonstrate initial success?

What will be put in place, when, by whom and how?

Structured opportunities for learning

Modelling/encouragement/reinforcement

Self-concept development

Relationship building

Other

How will the plan be monitored?

Review date (approximately six weeks)

Outcome of review

Decision following review

Continue with current plan/amend plan/change focus/seek further advice/other?

Chapter 8

Working with families

Parents almost always want the best for their children, even if they are unsure what that is or how to provide it. They do what they can as parents with the knowledge, skills, resources and support available to them. This includes personal resources. This chapter outlines what is involved in establishing and maintaining positive interactions with parents where there is a concern about behaviour. Assumption, judgement and blame are roads to nowhere. Early years practitioners can make all the difference to the development of parental confidence and competence but the communication process requires high levels of interpersonal skill. Working effectively with parents may provide our best chance of success with challenging children, especially in the development of more positive parent–child relationships.

This chapter is informed by research focusing on what parents found supportive in home–school interactions when behaviour was a concern (Roffey 2002 and 2004b).

TALKING ABOUT FAMILIES

It is a common discourse that children with challenging behaviour must have 'inadequate' or 'uncaring' families. If children are 'out of control' it must be that their parents 'let them get away with it' or 'can't be bothered to manage them properly'. How parents are discussed in the staffroom will have an impact on how they are seen, how their actions are interpreted and on the home–school interactions that follow. Many assumptions can be made about why children are not conforming to expectations, and reactions based on biased or incomplete information can lead to breakdown in relationships. When this happens, everyone loses out.

> *Cameron's mother died when he was just a baby and it was assumed for a long time that this was the reason for his difficulties. We now know that he is on the autistic spectrum.*
>
> *I was a single mum and I felt they were blaming my son's behaviour on this – but my daughter who was in the junior school had no problems.*

Rather than helplessly throw up our hands with 'it's his background – what can you do?' it is more useful to develop a constructive way of talking about families and children that offers possible solutions. Whatever we say about others includes our own perceptions and interpretations. No picture is 'objective' and it is helpful to acknowledge this.

THINKING ABOUT FAMILIES

All we can know about families is what they are prepared to communicate. The more information we are given about someone's situation the better able we may be to understand. We are, however, unlikely to ever be in the position of 'knowing everything' and this fact may perhaps enable us to reserve judgement.

Many parents with young children will be young themselves, perhaps inexperienced and struggling with other issues. They may be unprepared for the responsibilities that face them and not have support systems in place. Some are remarkable in their abilities to cope; others need sensitive guidance and emotional backing to optimize a developing sense of competence.

Parents may resort to 'authoritarian' or 'permissive' approaches because they don't know what else to do or do not have the emotional support which encourages them to think through how they interact with their children. Telling them they are wrong or giving them the impression they are bad parents will not change this. Modelling alternatives helps.

Other parents are so needy themselves that they cannot form an appropriate attachment with their child (see Chapter 6). Helping them find small joys in parenting is a start. This includes their own importance.

Some families are more experienced but faced with a child who is 'different'. Their knowledge about parenting and earlier confidence in their parental role is thrown into doubt. These parents need good information and reassurance.

Others are in a cultural cleft stick. They are parenting in ways in which they were parented and finding that this is somehow not working in a multi-cultural context. Families may be reluctant to relinquish traditions that give them a sense of belonging to their community. Giving clear information about your centre's approach to children enables new ideas to be discussed without making judgements on others.

Some parents, often mothers, have to cope with issues that leave them little energy to relate to or manage their children well. These stresses can include domestic violence, inadequate housing, health concerns, frequent mobility, caring for others, lack of social support, financial worries, racism and harassment. These parents need understanding and good information about available services and community support.

If adults have emotional traumas themselves, such as broken relationships, they may not have sufficient emotional resources to tune into their children's needs. The impact of family breakdown often has behavioural repercussions for small children and this is not often mediated well because parents are very needy themselves and do not know how best to talk to their children. Occasional workshops on 'loss' may help everyone (see Chapter 6).

Professional parents may have less time for their children than the children need; or they may keep them up late in the evening to see them. The children are then tired and irritable the next morning. This is tricky. Giving parents developmental information from time to time and ensuring that families are given good notice of any performance events so that they can put these in their diaries may be a start. Perhaps some written guidance on how to maximize the *quality* of child–parent interaction and suggestions about how to involve the children in some of their activities to foster both their learning and the relationship might also help. You might want to consider the occasional Saturday morning workshop if this is a real issue in your centre and you only ever see the au pair during the week.

Some parents are so keen for their children to 'succeed' that they have unrealistic and developmentally inappropriate expectations. They may not appreciate what is normal active behaviour in a pre-schooler. Explanation of how activities promote learning foundations may tune into the parents' concerns while protecting the child.

It would be foolish to deny that there are parents who do neglect or actively harm their children. Some are mentally ill, some have lives blighted by addictions and others do not have sufficient understanding of children or of themselves to know how to meet even minimum standards of 'good enough' parenting. These individuals may have had difficult childhoods themselves and developed few behavioural boundaries. Occasionally, parents appear to find something objectionable in one of their children and single this child out for particularly negative treatment (Harskamp 2002).

Abusive behaviour towards children is deeply disturbing to most people and this would especially be the case for those who have chosen to work as caring early years educators. Strong feelings may be felt towards the perpetrators. Working with abusive parents is therefore highly challenging for professionals. Buchanan (1996) says that it is an instinctive reaction to 'pathologize and marginalize the abuser'. Protecting the child from 'significant harm', however, means finding ways of working constructively with such families to achieve optimal outcomes. This is important both for the immediate situation and for the future (Department of Health 1999). There is evidence to suggest that the parent–child relationship can be both enhanced and damaged by what others say and how it is said.

The suggestions and framework for 'plugging into partnership' given here apply to all parents and carers of young children although the specifics may differ according to circumstances.

Teachers and parents see the same child through a different lens. The aim is to facilitate 'co-constructing' a view of the child that everyone can work with. This will only happen if the focus is on the *child* rather than the 'problem'.

ESTABLISHING RELATIONSHIPS IN THE BEGINNING

It is valuable for parents to understand what goes on in the centre and the rationale behind policies. Communicating philosophy, principles and practice about children's learning, behaviour and development will make a difference, not only to parents' understanding, but also the possibility that they might take some of your ideas home with them. A visual presentation, photographs or video of interactions in the nursery illustrating what you do and why is even better.

Smacking is a contentious issue. Some families believe they have a duty to discipline their children in this way. Without being judgemental explain why you consider this is not the best way of encouraging pro-social behaviour, perhaps using the information given in Chapter 2.

If you want parents to be willing to talk about difficulties it is essential they feel comfortable with you. Messages need to be welcoming and confirm the parent's role and competence. You can do this in several ways:

▶ Positive verbal and non-verbal greetings – say hello, smile and have a brief conversation about something other than their children.

▶ Encouragement to participate in various activities – without making anyone feel guilty if they don't.

▶ Sharing attention with all parents rather than just interacting with a few.

▶ Feeding back any positive developments for individual children. This is especially important as it reflects an interest in and concern for the whole child.

STAFF RAISING CONCERNS

Some teachers believe that parents need evidence of how difficult their child is and go about gathering this so that they can 'prove' their point. This is a waste of valuable time. Either the parents feel embarrassed, ashamed or inadequate or placed in a position in which they are obliged to defend their child. Alternatively parents may not see their child like that but agree with everything that is being said in order to maintain their child's place in the centre. Another scenario is that the professionals and parents agree, but leave the child with no advocate.

Parents are likely to feel blamed and that judgements are being made about them. You may not know all of the circumstances that underpin the difficulties the child is presenting and it is vital not to jump to conclusions. There may be loss, trauma, mental illness, violence or learning difficulties that are neglected in the quick and easy attribution of 'inadequate parenting'.

Parents may also feel that they are expected to 'take responsibility' for their child and do something to 'make the problem go away'. They may be at a loss themselves and don't know what to do, let alone be able to do it. Feeling inadequate does not foster partnership.

So what do you do? An informal approach that promotes the idea of complementary knowledge and gives priority to 'listening' rather than 'telling' and solutions rather than problems will be more productive. This will promote better relationships as well as improved understanding.

Discussions with parents need to take into account how they see themselves in their parental role, what they want for their child and what contextual factors need to be taken into consideration in planning intervention.

The first approaches could go something like this – it is less alarming for parents if concerns are raised gently over several conversations rather than all at once:

▶ Chat informally and indirectly. Include something positive about the child in question: *How is Finn going? He is such an independent little boy. What does he say about the centre?*

▶ Say that you are having a bit of a struggle and would like some ideas about what might work: *I don't know what to do when Finn gets frustrated. He just gets beside himself if things don't go right. Is he like that at home? What do you do?*

▶ Acknowledge that the parent is the expert on their own child (see p. 129). The parent may not realize her own level of expertise until you ask the questions that illustrate that depth of knowledge. Such a conversation may also trigger confidence and increased interest in the child's development and abilities.

▶ Listen to what the parent has to say – don't interrupt but reflect back what she is telling you and check that you have understood. You may find that the parent is worried about similar things. If you are able to share problems and solutions this provides practical and emotional support for both of you.

▶ If you feel it appropriate ask if there have been any changes at home that might have affected the child. If you have already established a trusting relationship the parent may feel safe in confiding. Do not, however, pry unnecessarily. Make sure parents know that you will not break confidentiality unless it becomes apparent that the child is in danger, in which case you are obliged by law to tell the person in your centre responsible for child protection.

▶ Ask about exceptions. When does this behaviour not occur? What seems to help the child manage his feelings? What has the parent done that has helped the child be happier or more in control? This focuses on strengths and competencies. If you simply ask what works you may just find out about punishments. If that is the case ask if this works in the longer term or if he does it again. Punishment is often used because of a lack of knowledge about strategies to promote wanted behaviour.

▶ Say what you will try: *I thought I might talk to Finn about what happens in his body when he feels himself beginning to get upset. Perhaps he could think of what would stop this feeling getting the better of him.*

▶ At this point make a definite arrangement to speak with the parent again so you can let her know how your intervention is going.

▶ When you meet again talk about what you are doing and its impact: *Finn is beginning to take some control of that temper. I told him how proud I was of him. I have also suggested that he says to himself 'This is going wrong and I can stamp my foot once to show how cross I am.' When I hear the stamp one of us goes over and helps him stay cool. It's working well.*

▶ Ask if the parent has noticed any difference at home since the last meeting.

▶ Ask the parent if they would like a brief chat once a week or so just to keep an eye on things and share ideas.

Within a trusting relationship, parents may want to talk to you about their own difficulties. In those discussions take into account what is important and relevant for them, how they feel about themselves in the parenting role and what is helpful in developing their confidence. If the parent becomes too demanding of your time, however, make time-limited appointments and/or see if you can refer them onto a counselling service.

PARENTS RAISING CONCERNS

Parents sometimes want to talk about concerns for their child but find it hard to do. They may not know what to say or how to say it, may feel intimidated by professionals or believe they have to be aggressive in order to be assertive. This has the potential to set up conflicts. Try not to take an 'inappropriate' approach personally but acknowledge the concern. A blanket reassurance that the child is progressing well may give the impression that you are not taking parents seriously. Even if you say that you have not noticed anything amiss add that you will make some closer observations or ask others and then arrange to meet again. If things are fine at home but not at the centre ask the parent why they

THE PARENT AS EXPERT ON THEIR OWN CHILDREN

These are things parents/carers may know which you may find helpful in constructing solutions:

▶ the child's history from birth: developmental, social, family and medical;

▶ aspects of the child's personality; their idiosyncrasies and their strengths;

▶ how they respond in different situations and with different family members;

▶ what their child can do and is just beginning to do at home;

▶ what they struggle with and what comes easily;

▶ what holds their interest and attention;

▶ what they like to do and do not like doing;

▶ how independent and determined they are;

▶ what comforts and soothes them;

▶ what distresses them;

▶ ways in which they try to communicate;

▶ what influences their motivation or mood;

▶ the circumstances in which they are most cooperative and/or confident;

▶ the circumstances in which they are most defiant or anxious;

▶ the circumstances in which they are best able to focus and concentrate;

▶ what supports their learning.

The answers to some of the above will help present the child's view. This puts the parent in the role of advocate for her child. Some parents may not realize this and value the concept offered. This fact-finding conversation (possibly several conversations) also raises ways for parents to be tuned into their child at home.

feel their child is not progressing well. If professionals stay open-minded it may provide an opportunity to improve on practice.

In all cases ensure that the parent is given copies of relevant policies which you may be referring to in the future.

LONGER-TERM NEEDS

The chapter on learning and language makes it clear that a high percentage of children whose behaviour does not respond to consistent positive interventions may have longer-term special educational needs. Sometimes this will be minor; sometimes it will be more serious. The impact on families when they realize that their child is 'different' cannot be over-estimated. What is being presented to them is the loss of the hopes, dreams and expectations they hold for their child. Many parents also feel guilty and believe this is somehow their fault.

The realization their child has learning difficulties can be devastating for some families while others experience relief that there is a reason for their many anxieties, especially when behaviour has been both challenging and puzzling. Some people deal better with what they know, others would prefer not to know.

Early years professionals cannot make parents 'see the obvious'. They need time to come to this understanding themselves. It is particularly hard where a child's special need is not immediately apparent. A communication or learning difficulty may be harder to come to terms with than disabilities that are more immediately visible. Some parents initially refuse to have any assessments and this can be frustrating to those who know that early intervention can make a difference to the eventual outcome. There is nothing you can do except to leave the door open for parents and do your best for the child in the meantime. Some families are worried their child will be labelled and categorized. They may be more prepared to discuss their child's progress if you do not write anything down. Keep your meetings action focused – tell parents what you are doing to help their child make progress and let them know all the incremental steps that are achieved. Focus discussions primarily around learning and not the child's problematic behaviour (Roffey 2001).

All meetings need to conclude as positively as possible with agreed actions. These could include:

▶ carry out some more formal observations to identify what the child can do and the circumstances in which she can do it;

▶ contact other professionals who may already be involved;

▶ ask for a consultation with a professional such as an educational psychologist;

▶ refer to others as appropriate such as a speech therapist;

▶ devise a home–school programme.

Setting a date for a review six weeks ahead gives time to put these actions in place.

HOME–SCHOOL PROGRAMMES

These will only work well if they are developed jointly with parents. Families may otherwise agree to do things that are not possible for them in reality. Their own circumstances, understanding and commitment will determine what happens. It is better to devise a joint plan that is minimal but workable. Focus on what will raise the parent's confidence and improve the relationship with her child.

MORE FORMAL MEETINGS

These meetings will occur when something has already been put in place to address the child's needs. Part of the discussion will be related to the effectiveness of any programme and what this has indicated about continuing needs.

A formal meeting may include other professionals but should still be focused on what can be done to support the child and family.

If good practice has taken place parents will already know the purpose of the meeting. A request to attend such a discussion out of the blue raises unnecessary anxiety. They also need to know how long it will last and who will be there. An invitation to bring along a friend or family member provides support and also facilitates recall. Sometimes parents become overwhelmed and are not able to attend to everything that is said.

It demonstrates respect if meetings are not interrupted by knocks or phone calls. A notice on the door and the phone off the hook (or set up for messages) will help. Meetings should start and end on time and childcare needs taken into consideration.

The full participation of parents requires that everyone is on equal terms. This means sitting together (without one person behind a desk) and everyone using the same mode of address, usually first names. Some meetings will require interpreting services but all need to avoid specific jargon. Phrases and acronyms that are part of everyday professional communication may mean nothing to those outside early years education. Giving family members papers to read in a meeting assumes that they are literate in the English language: that may not be the case. It is also difficult to absorb information under such circumstances. It is vital that parents' views are elicited, listened to and taken seriously. They should also be given opportunities to ask questions and to clarify anything they don't fully understand.

Someone needs to take notes at formal meetings to ensure that everyone is agreed on what should be happening next and who is going to be doing what.

ESTABLISHING A SYSTEMIC SOLUTION-FOCUSED SPIRAL

Despite our desire for a simple cause-and-effect attribution for behaviour, life and human beings are usually more complex. Many interactive factors over time may have resulted in a problematic downward spiral. There is only so much early years practitioners can do to reverse this but a systemic analysis will tell you that actions you take and things you say may have more impact than you can imagine. Here is a simple example of the interactions between systems and what a constructive way of thinking might achieve:

- ► early years practitioner sets up a 'success opportunity' – something where the child will be guaranteed to achieve;
- ► parent is given positive messages about child's good (or improved) behaviours;
- ► practitioner attributes this success to positive qualities in the child (important);
- ► parent sees child more positively – tells extended family about progress;
- ► parent and extended family focus on identified progress;
- ► progress reinforced;
- ► parent–child relationship enhanced;
- ► parent more confident and more willing to listen to early years staff;
- ► practitioner does not tell parent what to do but gives information about what she is doing which is effective;

- ▶ parent is also asked for her ideas;
- ▶ parent is therefore not undermined and feels acknowledged;
- ▶ home–centre relationship strengthened;
- ▶ parenting competency and confidence developed;
- ▶ parent's contribution to improvements acknowledged.

Even if the child's needs continue at a high level this respectful approach ensures that optimal outcomes occur for everyone.

SUMMARY

Working collaboratively with parents/carers is likely to be our best chance of success in ameliorating behavioural difficulties. In the early years this is especially crucial. There is a high level of intra- and inter-personal skills required. These, however, will only be translated into practice when both parents and children are positioned as part of the solution rather than part of the problem.

Chapter 9

Looking after yourself and each other

Young children are demanding at the best of times — those who are difficult to manage can be very draining. Low emotional energies mean that you react in ways that you know are not the best. Doing what you can to keep emotional resources topped up keeps things in perspective and maintains your professional integrity in caring for the children in your centre. Part of this is looking after yourself and the rest is the network of support in your workplace.

Children who are growing up in caring and supportive families can be exhausting – their energy levels and exuberance keep adults on their toes. Those who are distressed, difficult or defiant can be very wearing indeed. They challenge not only physical energy, but also emotional energy. When this is combined with other things not going well you can lose sight, not only of the best way of handling difficulties, but also of the simple enjoyment in your job. Being with young children can be very rewarding and pleasurable – it is important you stay in touch with this and get the most out of what you do. This chapter shows how to maintain your resources so you can focus on the positive and deal with the challenging in sensitive and confident ways.

PHYSICAL RESOURCES

No one performs at an optimal level when basic survival needs are not being met. Relieving cold, hunger and exhaustion and ensuring safety are priorities for attention. This applies to the children in your care but it also applies to you. Looking after yourself well provides the physical energy to stay on top of the job and stay emotionally literate. It is when you are tired, drained, distracted and under par that you snap and react to situations badly. Children and colleagues may be in the firing line of a hasty word or action and this is not good for anyone, including you. You are also less creative. Being able to think on your feet is a useful skill when faced with challenging children.

Ensure you have maximum energy and can operate at an optimum level by:

▶ getting enough good quality sleep;
▶ eating good food regularly;
▶ getting both exercise and relaxation.

All the above are interconnected. Together they put you on an upward spiral to increase both wellness and well-being. When you are physically very active your serotonin levels rise. This is the chemical neurotransmitter that makes you feel calmer and more in control. There is good evidence that physical activity also helps keep depression at bay. Exercise improves your circulation, gives you more energy and will also help you sleep better. Eating well gives you the energy you need.

If you have trouble going to sleep try a routine before bedtime to give yourself at least an hour of winding down. Worry stops you sleeping and also wakes you up in the early hours. Learn some relaxation and meditation techniques but if all else fails go and see your doctor or a counsellor. You cannot function well if you are exhausted, especially when dealing with little ones all day.

WEARY AT WORK

If you do find yourself occasionally weary at work then you need to conserve energy as much as possible but still be effective. So long as this is not a regular situation you could use this as a teaching opportunity to develop perspective-taking and empathy. It can be empowering for children to take responsibility and be 'in charge' for a change.

Tell the children you need their help today, as you are not feeling very well. Ask them what they might need if they are feeling unwell and talk about this. Ask individuals for specific help, like fetching something or helping the group become quiet. Give positive feedback about how much better they are making you feel.

135

This:

▶ raises the focus on perspective-taking;
▶ promotes consideration for others;
▶ tunes into emotional regulation about what makes us feel better;
▶ gives an opportunity to get positive feedback for helping;
▶ raises self-efficacy in children – they are making a difference.

When you know your resources are low you need to pay particular attention to slowing down reactions to challenges. Then you are less likely to do something you later regret.

EMOTIONAL RESOURCES

We know when emotional resources are worryingly low. We are edgy, out of sorts, possibly weepy, anxious and reactive. It is most evident when we know the best way of handling a situation but find it hard to put into practice.

Emotional energies are drained when demands and stresses exceed the positives in our lives. It is amazing how much better we can cope when we feel valued, can share the load and have a different or more hopeful perspective. We need to look carefully at what is undermining us and how we can reduce this impact, what is already in place to raise our resources and what we might do in addition.

HELPING YOURSELF

Be aware of emotional triggers

It is useful to know what really gets to you and winds you up. This is different for everyone. Once you are aware you can take evasive action or develop prior responses for use in challenging situations. Explosions and constant irritations deplete emotional energy. If something over-whelms you emotionally avoid making decisions on the spot if you can – wait until you can 'think straight'.

Emotional regulation

There are times you may feel particularly low. You need to be able to regulate your emotional state more actively than just regular relaxation. Work out what makes you feel better but does not make things worse in the longer term. Some people try to feel better in ways that are ultimately damaging to themselves or others.

Positive mood enhancers include music, good company, physical activity, books, films and other media, warmth and affection, planning good times ahead and becoming absorbed in something you enjoy that takes up mental space.

Thinking

The way you think about your job, yourself in it and the children who challenge will have an impact on your emotional resources. Some ways of thinking lead to helplessness and hopelessness, others to a sense of fulfilment in what you are doing.

You can position children in many different ways. Think of a child who is screaming at you and refusing to have any help putting on her boots. You could 'position' her as disruptive, independent, oppositional, uncooperative, determined, defiant, expressive, spirited, insolent, difficult, lacking guidance, aggressive, having a tough day or hard-to-manage. There are many other potential constructs. How you position the child will imply how you are positioned yourself and the action you take:

- ▶ If you see her as disruptive then you position yourself as responsible for maintaining order.
- ▶ If you see her as determined you could consider yourself responsible for developing her strengths in socially acceptable ways.
- ▶ If independent – you will be focusing on developmental expectations and acknowledging her drive for autonomy.
- ▶ If defiant – perhaps you consider you need to re-assert control.
- ▶ If aggressive – your focus may be on protecting others.
- ▶ If insolent – you may consider that you have to defend yourself.
- ▶ If you position her as having a disorder then she is seen as 'not normal' and you may focus on her differences rather than what she has in common with other children.
- ▶ If you see her as having a tough day then perhaps you will be looking at how to make it better.

Same behaviour, same child but the interpretation you make determines what you do and how you do it. You may choose several. There is no right or wrong here but some will take up more emotional energy than others. What is congruent with your values and in the best interests of the child? Which ways of thinking lead you to develop ways of being and doing which encourage learning and development and give positive ideas for intervention?

There is increasing evidence to connect positive thinking with well-being (Frederickson *et al.* 2000). Among other things this means acknowledging mistakes and learning from them but *not* beating yourself up and giving yourself 'I am useless' messages. Be firm with the negative voices in your head and try to make positive choices in thinking, both for yourself and the children you work with. Maintain a focus on what you have achieved, however small.

Use time well

Time is finite. We cannot have more of it so we need to make the best of what we have. Some planning is helpful. Spend half an hour a week writing down what you need to fit in (bearing in mind what is currently *not* necessary) and when. It does not help to be too rigid – build in flexibility – and also put regular time aside for relaxation. At what level of perfection are you aiming? Some things need to be done to a high standard, others less so. Work out your priorities.

Planning for behaviour

Many educators say that responding to behavioural difficulties is time consuming. You can cut down this unplanned demand if you pre-empt difficulties in the first place by promoting the positive. It also saves time and emotional energy if you know what to put in place when things do not go well.

Personal support

This comes in several guises:

> ▶ People who are there to guide you professionally and help out with things you don't know. This might be your line manager or a peer with more experience. Identify who you can go to if you are uncertain about something. Do not engage with those who

CASE STUDY

Vanessa was asked to write an assessment report on one of the children in the centre. She took this very seriously and wrote a report that covered the child's history from the day of enrolment and everything that was worrying about her progress. She included detailed examples of 'evidence' from memory. The report ran to twelve pages and took her a whole weekend to write. Although everyone appreciated the effort she could have encapsulated the vital information in two or three pages, summarized the actions taken and identified the ongoing needs. A shorter, more succinct report would also have taken less time to read and presented a clearer focus for planning.

---

are negative or cynical if you can avoid it. These attitudes undermine your emotional resources and do not help with positive problem-solving.

▶ Friends and family who provide you with emotional support. If you are really struggling either spread the load around or go and see a counsellor. It puts pressure on friendship if demands for support and listening become one-sided.

▶ Friends who do not necessarily provide direct emotional support but who are fun to be with and take you out of yourself. If you feel better about life after an evening with them they are to be treasured.

If you are not getting to spend time with the people who are important to you then think of them as appointments – it is surprising how we can always get to an appointment!

Relaxation

Relaxation is more than doing things away from work. It is doing whatever revives you physically, mentally and emotionally. This means doing things that you love to do, that give you a sense of deep satisfaction and clear your head. Even if it is only for fifteen minutes a day be good to yourself. Not only do you deserve it but so do the children you work with. Plan for it. A burnt-out teacher is no fun.

Having fun

Sometimes we get ourselves into a place where we do not seek creative alternatives to our thinking. This means that we have increasing thoughts along the lines of: 'this child is making too many demands' or 'I am not going to let this bossy one dictate what I do today' or 'I have too many things to get through to listen to this'. Sometimes choosing a more light-hearted, creative and positive response can give everyone a lot of fun and strengthen relationships. So long as it is congruent with your basic principles for behaviour let the children take the lead sometimes, make a game instead of a demand, go with the flow and be flexible.

HELPING EACH OTHER

The culture in which you work has a significant impact on your sense of well-being. Where there is a sense of belonging individuals do not feel isolated and know they have back-up in challenging situations. People also feel more energized, collegial and positive when their efforts are acknowledged and valued. Valuing each other does not have to be a major event. Just the occasional thanks and *I noticed that . . .* is enough.

 CASE STUDY

One staff group had a circle-time meeting in which each person put their name in a hat and drew out the name of a colleague. This was the name of their 'secret friend' for the week. The idea was to do something to make this person feel valued in some way. The following week staff talked about their experience. Actions included putting little thank you notes or small gifts such as a wrapped chocolate in their pigeonhole. Everyone said it had given them a boost, whether they had identified their 'secret friend' or not.

Supportive conversations

A supportive conversation is constructive, not destructive; solution focused not problem focused. It is where someone can safely admit they

WHAT WORKS FOR ME		
	What I already do/have	What else might help?
Looking after my physical needs – sleep, exercise, eating well		
Looking after my emotional needs 1: Relaxation and being good to myself		
Looking after my emotional needs 2: Network of support		
Time management		
Useful ways of thinking		

DEVELOPING A POSITIVE BEHAVIOUR POLICY

1 Discuss your values as a staff.

2 Agree which values and principles will underpin your policy.

3 Give everyone in the school and the community the opportunity to say which behaviours should be encouraged. This includes the children.

4 A small team of volunteers draws up a draft document aimed at promoting positive behaviour.

   This draft document will include:

   ▶ A statement of basic values/principles – what is seen as important?

   ▶ A statement of basic aims – what do you want this policy to achieve?

   ▶ A brief list of behaviours that the centre is encouraging – these are likely to be non-specific at this point, e.g. 'be fair'.

   ▶ The rationale for this list so everyone can understand why each behaviour is included.

   ▶ A statement of how these behaviours will be:
      - modelled;
      - taught directly;
      - otherwise promoted.

5 In order to clarify from the general to the specific, the policy will say that these behaviours will be high profile and regularly discussed by both staff and children. Words such as 'kind' and 'friendly' require constant input so that everyone knows what they mean in practice. Positive behaviour policies need to be alive on a daily basis.

   The policy will also include:

   ▶ A statement of what a staff member might do and say when a child does something that is hurtful.

▶ A statement of what a staff member might do and say when a child does something that is unhelpful.

What will happen if a child's behaviour is regularly hard to manage:

▶ how parents will be involved as partners;

▶ how assessments will be carried out and programmes developed;

▶ what the procedures will be for monitoring and review.

6 This draft policy is then given out to all stakeholders for their comments. Meetings are held in small groups so that parents can be closely involved in the development. This provides an excellent opportunity for sharing developmental understanding and good practice in behavioural issues with families without de-skilling them. Children are also involved at the appropriate level.

7 The final policy is drawn up.

8 This substantive document is given to all new parents in an intake meeting where it is explained in detail. It is also given to new members of staff.

9 Each new child is introduced to the expected behaviours by the teacher and by the established group. The older children are encouraged to help the younger children learn by showing them what to do and how to do it.

10 The policy is reviewed twice a year at a whole staff meeting. Amendments and adaptations are discussed and incorporated if they are in line with the original values and principles.

11 A values exercise is also revisited every two years to ensure that there is consistency and consensus.

have a difficulty. A supportive colleague listens without being judgemental, is empathic but offers fresh perspectives and is helpful without being de-skilling. Do not participate in discourses that are negative, cynical and blaming. These are more likely to reduce optimism, limit creativity and foster depression.

Supportive management   A supportive management is interested, not only in running an efficient and effective centre, but also in the well-being of the staff. Supportive managers are clear about their philosophy and communicate that with everyone. They are available and approachable and do not jump to conclusions without hearing all sides of a situation. Democratic practices where staff are consulted in decision making are more likely to have consistency and commitment to policy. (If you are not so fortunate with your line manager see 'personal support' above.)

Behaviour policies   Having a behaviour policy can be a straitjacket or a useful working document. This is a blueprint for the development of a positive behaviour policy. Don't expect to do this overnight. The process is as important as the content. This is described on pp. 142–3.

AND FINALLY, WAYS TO STAY POSITIVE

It is useful to think about the incremental gains that children make in developing social, emotional and behavioural skills. Each step is to be celebrated, however small, both with the child and with their parents. Take credit yourself for what has worked.

Start a file of positive events, stories and feedback. These will refresh your spirit when you are down.

If things get really difficult imagine you are watching a film. This keeps your worst feelings at bay and helps you not take things personally.

Use your feelings productively to help you understand and empathize with some of your most challenging children.

Keep a light-hearted view and look for moments of warmth and laughter. There are so many to be had in the early years. Sometimes you can choose to see the funny side.

CASE STUDY

Evie found a handbag, opened the handbag and found the lovely make-up. Evie had seen her mummy use this stuff. When Evie next appeared she had lipstick and eye shadow in all the right and all the wrong places. There were several possible options here – explain very carefully to Evie that she was never to open anyone's handbag ever again, focus on just how much had been ruined (the cosmetics themselves, not to mention Evie's dress and the handbag) or howl with laughter – just this once! Handbags stayed out of reach after that though and the only face painting that was allowed happened at the fair.

SUMMARY

If you are having an enjoyable time at work, then it is more likely that you will be positive, creative, empathic and calm with the children, however challenging they are. Your job as an early years professional is vital, your professional integrity essential. You owe it to yourself and to the children to maximize your own well-being.

Bibliography

Antidote (2003) *The Emotional Literacy Handbook: Promoting Whole-school Strategies*, London: David Fulton Publishers.

Atwater, J.B. and Morris, E.K. (1988) 'Teachers' instructions and children's compliance in pre-school classrooms: a descriptive analysis', *Journal of Applied Behaviour Analysis*, 21 (2): 157–67.

Bandura, A. (1971) *Social Learning Theory*, New York: General Learning Press.

Baumrind, D. (1971) 'Current patterns of parental authority', *Developmental Psychology Monograph*, 4: 1–103.

Benner, G., Nelson, J. and Epstein, M. (2002) 'Language skills of children with EBD: a literature review', *Journal of Emotional and Behavioural Disorders*, 10 (1): 43–59.

Billington, T. (2000) *Separating, Losing and Excluding Children: Narratives of Difference*, London and New York: RoutledgeFalmer.

Bluestein, J. (2001) *Creating Emotionally Safe Schools: A Guide for Educators and Parents*, Florida: Health Communications Inc.

Bowlby, J. (1973) *Attachment and Loss, Vol. 2: Separation, Anxiety and Anger*, London: Penguin.

Bronfenbrenner, U. (1979) *The Ecology of Human Development: Experiments by Nature and Design*, Cambridge, MA: Harvard University Press.

—— (2004) *Making Human Beings Human: Bioecological Perspectives on Human Development*, London and Thousand Oaks, CA: Sage Publications.

Brown, E. (1999) *Loss, Change and Grief: An Educational Perspective*, London: David Fulton Publishers.

Buchanan, A. (1996) *Cycles of Child Maltreatment: Facts, Fallacies and Intervention*, Chichester: Wiley.

Campbell Rightmyer, E. (2003) 'Democratic discipline: children creating solutions', *Young Children*, July 2003: 38–45.

Canter, L. (1992) *Assertive Discipline*, Santa Monica, CA: Lee Canter and Associates.

Clough, P. and Nutbrown, C. (2004) 'Special educational needs and inclusion: multiple perspectives of pre-school educators in the UK', *Journal of Early Childhood Research*, 2 (2): 191–211.

Collins, E. and McGaha, C. (2002) 'Create rewarding circle times by working with toddlers, not against them', *Childhood Education*, 78 (4): 194–9.

Collins, M. (2001) *Circle Time for the Very Young*, Bristol: Lucky Duck Publishers.

Cross, M. (2004) *Children with Emotional and Behavioural Difficulties and Communication Problems*, London and New York: Jessica Kingsley Publishers.

Denham, S.A. (1996) 'Pre-schoolers understanding of parents' emotions: implications for emotional competence', unpublished manuscript cited in Denham, S.A. (1998) *Emotional Development in Young Children*, New York and London: Guilford Press.

—— (1998) *Emotional Development in Young Children*, New York and London: Guilford Press.

—— and Zoller, D. (1991) '"When my hamster died, I cried": pre-schoolers' attributions of the causes of emotions', *Journal of Genetic Psychology*, 152: 371–3.

Department for Education and Employment (1998) *Education for citizenship and democracy in schools* (The Crick Report). Final report of the Advisory Group on Citizenship London: Qualifications and Curriculum Authority.

Department for Education and Skills: www.teachernet.gov.uk, accessed September 2004.

Department of Health (1999) *Working Together to Safeguard Children*, London: The Stationery Office.

Depue, R., Luciana, M., Arbisi, P., Collins, P. and Leon, A. (1994) 'Dopamine and the structure of personality: relation of agonist-induced dopamine activity to positive emotionality', *Journal of Personality and Social Psychology*, 67: 486–98.

Dockett, S. and Perry, B. (2004) 'Starting school: perspectives of Australian children, parents and educators', *Journal of Early Childhood Research*, 2 (2): 171–89.

Dowling, E. and Gorell Barnes, G. (2000) *Working with Children and Parents through Separation and Divorce*, Basingstoke: Macmillan.

Dowling, M. (2000) *Young Children's Personal, Social and Emotional Development*, London and Thousand Oaks, CA: Paul Chapman Publishing/Sage Publications.

Doyle, R. (2003) 'Developing the nurturing school: Spreading nurture group principles and practices into mainstream classes', *Emotional and Behavioural Difficulties*, 8 (4): 252–66.

Dunn, J. (1993) *Young Children's Close Relationships: Beyond Attachment*, London and Thousand Oaks, CA: Sage Publications.

—— and Hughes, C. (2001) '"I got some swords and you're dead": violent fantasy, antisocial behaviour, friendship and moral sensibility in young children', *Child Development*, 72 (2): 491–505.

Eisenberg, N., Fabes, R., Murphy, B., Karbon, M., Smith, M. and Masck, P. (1996) 'The relations of children's dispositional empathy-related responding to their emotionality, regulation and social functioning', *Developmental Psychology*, 32: 195–209.

—— , Losoya, S. and Guthrie, I.K. (1997) 'Social cognition and pro-social development', in Hala, S. (ed.) *The Development of Social Cognition*: 329–63, East Sussex: Psychology Press.

Farver, J.M. (1996) 'Aggressive behaviour in pre-schoolers' social networks: do birds of a feather flock together?', *Early Childhood Research Quarterly*, 11 (3): 333–50.

Foot, H., Woolfson, L., Terras, M. and Norfolk, C. (2004) 'Handling hard-to-manage behaviours in pre-school provision: a systems approach', *Journal of Early Childhood Research*, 2 (2): 115–38.

Fox, L., Dunlap, G., Hemmeter, M.L., Joseph, G. and Strain, P. (2003) 'The teaching pyramid: a model for supporting social competence and preventing challenging behaviour in young children', *Young Children*, July 2003: 48–52.

Frederickson, B. and Tugade, M. (2004) 'Resilient individuals use positive emotions to bounce back from negative emotional experiences', *Journal of Personality and Social Psychology*, 86 (2): 320–33.

—— , Mancuso, R., Branigan, C. and Tugade, M. (2000) 'The undoing effect of positive emotion', *Motion and Emotion*, 24 (4): 237–44.

Geddes, H, (2003) 'Attachment and the child in school', *Emotional and Behavioural Difficulties*, 8 (3): 231–42.

Gerhardt, S. (2004) *Why Love Matters: How affection shapes a baby's brain*, Hove and New York: Bruner Routledge.

Gilligan, C. and Wiggins, G. (1988) 'The origins of morality in early childhood relationships', in Gilligan, C., Ward, J. and Taylor, J. (eds) *Mapping the Moral Domain*, Cambridge, MA: Harvard University Press.

Goleman, D. (1996) *Emotional Intelligence: Why it Can Matter More Than I.Q.*, London: Bloomsbury Press.

Gray, C. (2002) *My Social Stories Book*. Online. Available http://www.thegray center.org (accessed 1 November 2004).

Gronlund, G. (1992) 'Coping with ninja turtle play in my kindergarten classroom', *Young Children*, 48 (1): 21–25.

Harding, J. and Pribam, E. (2002) 'The power of feeling: locating emotions in culture', *European Journal of Cultural Studies*, 5 (4): 407–26.

Harrist, A. and Bradley, K.D. (2003) '"You can't say you can't play": intervening in the process of social exclusion in the kindergarten classroom', *Early Childhood Research Quarterly*, 18: 185–205.

Harskamp, A. (2002) 'Working with parents who harm their children', in Roffey, S. (ed.) *School Behaviour and Families*, London: David Fulton Publishers.

Hinshaw, S.P. (1992) 'Externalising problems and academic underachievement in childhood and adolescence: causal relationships and underlying mechanisms', *Psychological Bulletin*, 111 (1): 127–55.

Hoffman, J. (1999) 'Great expectations: when discipline and development clash, here's how to sort out what's misbehaviour and what's age appropriate', *Today's Parent*, 16 (4): 42.

Hoffman, M.L. (1988) 'Moral development', in Bernstein, M.H. and Lamb, M.E. (eds) *Developmental Psychology: an advanced textbook*, 2nd edn: 497–548, Mahwah, NJ: Erlbaum.

Holland, P. (2003) *We Don't Play with Guns Here: War, Weapon and Superhero Play in the Early Years*, Maidenhead: Open University Press.

Horsch, P., Chen, J. and Wagner, S. (2002) 'The responsive classroom approach: a caring, respectful school environment as a context for development', *Education and Urban Society*, 34 (3): 365–83.

Hromek, R. (2004) *Planting the Peace Virus: Early Intervention to Prevent Violence in Schools*, Bristol: Lucky Duck Publishers.

Hyson, M. (1994) *The Emotional Development of Young Children: Building an Emotion-Centred Curriculum*, New York and London: Teachers College Press.

Jones, L. (2001) 'Trying to break bad habits in practice by engaging with post-structuralist theories', *Early Years*, 21 (1): 25–32.

Joseph, G.E. and Strain, P. (2003) 'Comprehensive evidence based social-emotional curricula for young children: an analysis of efficacious adoption potential', *Topics in Early Childhood Special Education*, 2003, 23 (2): 65–76.

Kasser, T., Keostner, R. and Lekes, N. (2002) 'Early family experiences and adult values: a 26-year prospective longitudinal study', *Personality and Social Psychology Bulletin*, 28 (6): 826–35.

Katz, L.G. (1995) *Talks with teachers of young children*, Norwood, NJ: Ablex.

Kindlon, D. and Thompson, M. (1999) *Raising Cain: Protecting the Emotional Life of Boys*, London, New York and Ringwood Australia: Penguin Books.

Kochanska, G. (1991) 'Socialisation and temperament in the development of guilt and conscience', *Child Development*, 62: 1379–92.

Kohlberg, L. (1984) *Essays on Moral Development, Vol. 2: the psychology of moral development*, San Francisco: HarperCollins.

Laird, J. and Apostoleris, N. (1996) 'Emotional self-control and self-perception: feelings are the solution, not the problem', in Harre, R. and Parrott, W. (eds) *The Emotions: Social, Cultural and Biological Dimensions*, London: Sage Publications.

Laws, C. and Davies, B. (2000) 'Poststructuralist theory in practice: working with "behaviourally disturbed" children', *Qualitative Studies in Education*, 13 (3): 205–21.

Levin, D. (2003) 'Beyond banning war and superhero play: meeting children's needs in violent times', *Young Children*, May 2003: 60–3.

Maines, B. and Robinson, G. (1992) *Crying for Help: The No-blame Approach to Bullying*, Bristol: Lucky Duck Publishers.

Mapinga, E., Garrison, B. and Pierce, S. (2002) 'An exploratory study of the relationships between family functioning and parenting styles: the perceptions of mothers of young grade school children', *Family and Consumer Sciences Research Journal*, 31 (1): 112–29.

Maslow, A. (1954) *Motivation and Personality*, New York: Harper & Row.

Miller, J. (1996) *Never Too Young: How Young Children can Take Responsibility and Make Decisions*, London: National Early Years Network.

Monahon, C. (1993) *Children and Trauma*, New York: Lexington Books.

National Research Council and Institute of Medicine (2000) 'From neurons to neighbourhoods: the science of early childhood development. Committee on Integrating the Science of Early Childhood Development', in Schonkoff, J.P. and Phillips, D.A. (eds) *Board on Children, Youth and Families, Commission on Behavioural and Social Sciences and Education*, Washington, DC: National Academy Press.

New South Wales Department of Education and Training (1998) *HealthCare and Safety Matters in All Schools*, Sydney.

150

Owusu-Bempah, K. and Howitt, D. (2000) *Psychology Beyond Western Perspectives*, Leicester: British Psychological Society.

Paley, V. (1992) *You can't say you can't play*, Cambridge, MA: Harvard University Press.

Papatheodorou, T. (2000) 'Management approaches employed by teachers to deal with children's behaviour problems in nursery classes', *School Psychology International*, 21 (4): 415–40.

Piaget, J. (1965) *The Moral Judgement of the Child*, New York: Free Press (Original work published 1932).

Pianta, R. (ed.) (1992) *Beyond the Parent: The Role of Other Adults in Children's Lives*, San Francisco, CA: Jossey Bass.

Popov, N. (1995) *Why?* New York and London: North-South Books.

Porter, L. (1997) *Children Are People Too: a Parent's Guide to Young Children's Behaviour*, Adelaide: Small Poppies.

—— (2003) *Young Children's Behaviour: Practical Approaches for Caregivers and Teachers*, London and Thousand Oaks, CA: Paul Chapman Publishing/Sage Publications.

Raphael, B. (2000) *Promoting the Mental Health and Wellbeing of Children and Young People*, Canberra: National Mental Health Working Group, Department of Health and Aged Care.

Roffey, S. (2001) *Special Needs in the Early Years: Collaboration, Communication, Coordination*, London: David Fulton Publishers.

—— (ed.) (2002) *School Behaviour and Families: Frameworks for Working Together*, London: David Fulton Publishers.

—— (2004a) *The New Teacher's Survival Guide to Behaviour*, London and Thousand Oaks, CA: Paul Chapman Publishers/Sage Publications.

—— (2004b) 'The home–school interface for behaviour: Co-constructing reality', *Child and Educational Psychology*, 20 (4): 95–108.

——, Avenoso, C., Birrell, I., Nand, A. and Ticli, S. (2004c) 'Constructions of Hard to Manage Children in a Pre-school Centre', unpublished study, University of Western Sydney.

—— and O'Reirdan, T. (2001) *Young Children and Classroom Behaviour: Needs, Perspectives and Strategies*, London: David Fulton Publishers.

——, Tarrant, T. and Majors, K. (1994) *Young Friends: Schools and Friendship*, London: Cassell Education.

Rubin, Z. (1980) *Children's Friendships,* London: Open Books.

Saarni, C. (1999) *The Development of Emotional Competence*, New York and London: Guilford Press.

Salovey, P. and Sluyter, D. (eds) (1997) *Emotional Development and Emotional Intelligence: Educational Implications*, New York: Basic Books.

Selman, R.L. (1980) *The Growth of Interpersonal Understanding*, New York: Academic Press.

Steinberg, L., Darling, N., Fletcher, A. with Bradford Brown, B. and Dornbusch, S. (1995) 'Authoritative parenting and adolescent adjustment: an ecological journey', in Moen, P., Elder, G. and Luscher, K. *Examining Lives in Context: Perspectives on the Ecology of Human Development*: 423–66, Washington: American Psychological Association.

Stoel, C.F. and Thant, T.S. (2002) *Teachers' Professional Lives: a View from Nine Industrialised Countries*, Washington, DC: Milken Family Foundation.

Thompson, K.L. and Gullone, E. (2003) 'Promotion of empathy and pro-social behaviour in children through humane education', *Australian Psychologist*, 28 (3): 175–82.

Thurman, S., Cornwell, J. and Gottwald, S. (1997) *Contexts of Early Intervention: Systems and Settings*, Baltimore, MD: Paul Brookes.

Turner H.A. and Muller, P.A. (2004) 'Long-term effects of child corporal punishment on depressive symptoms in young adults', *Journal of Family Issues*, 25: 761–82.

Vygotsky L.S. (1978) *Mind in Society*, Cambridge, MA: Harvard University Press.

Watson, M. (2003) 'Attachment theory and challenging behaviours: reconstructing the nature of relationships', *Young Children*, July 2003: 12–20.

Weare, K. and Gray, G. (2003) 'What works in developing children's emotional and social competence and well being?', *Report for the Department of Education and Skills*, Southampton: The Health Education Unit, University of Southampton.

Weitzman, E. (1992) *Learning Language and Loving It*, Toronto: Hanen Centre.

Winslade, J. and Monk G. (1999) *Narrative Counselling in Schools*, Thousand Oaks, CA: Corwin Press.

Wolfendale, S. and Robinson, M. (2001) *Educational Psychologists Working with the Early Years: a Framework for Practice*, Stratford: University of East London.

Zeitlin, S. and Williamson, G. (1994) *Coping in Young Children: Early Intervention Practices to Enhance Adaptive Behaviour and Resilience*, Baltimore, MD: Paul Brookes Publishing.

Index

smacking 16, 73, 125
social behaviours 4, 16, 21, 26–7,
    36, 59–61, 104, 118
social construction 5–6
social exclusion 1, 63
solution-focused approach 1, 8, 40,
    45, 123, 126, 132, 140
strengths 2–3, 21, 61, 85, 102–3,
    127, 129, 137
superheroes 73
systems 4–5, 61, 123, 132–3

temper tantrum 55, 108–9
thinking 3–7, 68–9, 80, 91, 106,
    115, 123, 132, 137–40

time 10, 17, 21, 35, 43, 58,
    95, 113, 124, 126–8, 138–9
toileting 83, 116–18
trauma 3, 93, 98–101, 124,
    126
trust 12–13, 37, 57, 60, 101,
    115, 127–8

values 2–6, 17, 19–20, 23, 27, 38–9,
    52, 138, 142–3
violence 72, 98, 101, 124,
    126
visual narratives 90–2, 109

warmth 17, 60, 95, 137, 145

About *Nursery World*

Nursery World is the only weekly magazine for the childcare and early years education sector, and will keep you up to date with all the latest news, views and changes in government policy. Each week there are also advertisements for hundreds of job vacancies.

You'll find a wealth of practical content including:

- in-depth coverage of the Foundation Stage curriculum and Birth to Threes
- full projects plus ideas for outdoor activities, display and music.

The magazine also contains special eight-page 'All About . . .' guides on subjects such as learning through play, plus free posters.

There is also plenty of advice on working with parents, with guides and posters that can be photocopied or displayed for parents to read.

Other regular series provide information about good practice, child behaviour, inclusion, careers and training.

Nursery World also publishes a range of special supplements including Nursery Business, Nursery Equipment, Nursery Topics, Nursery Chains and Training Today.

You can buy *Nursery World* from your newsagent every Thursday – or take out a subscription by calling 0870 444 8628 or ordering online at www.nurseryworld.co.uk.